D1176009

Vacation at Sunshine Farm

June Jumps For Joy

Andrea Wandel

June Jumps For Joy

Translated by Karen Nickel Anhalt

Copyright: © Andrea Wandel 2009
Translated by Karen Nickel Anhalt
Original title: Ferien Auf Dem Sonnenhof #2:
Juli springt ins Glück
Cover and inside illustrations: © Eleonore Gerhaher
Cover layout: © Stabenfeldt AS
Typeset by Roberta L. Melzl
Editor: Bobbie Chase
Printed in Germany, 2009

Stabenfeldt, Inc.
225 Park Avenue South
New York, NY 10003
www.pony4kids.com

ISBN: 978-1-934983-19-5

Available exclusively through PONY.

Horseback riding camp in idyllic Upper Marlboro for boys and girls, 8-16 years of age. Affectionate care, exceptionally beautiful grounds for trail rides and riding instructions with well-trained ponies and horses guaranteed. Lodgings in our picturesque farmhouse. All guests will have their own horse or pony to care for. Contact: Marty Sunshyne, sunshine@horsemail.com, Tel. ...

Chapter 1

"Vacation at Sunshine Farm?" The husky blonde girl waved the magazine under Liane's nose.

"What kind of junk is this?"

"Give that back to me right now!" cried Liane. As she took a step in her direction, the other girl jumped away and laughed, teasing her.

"Come and get it yourself. Nyah nyah na nyah nyah."

Liane could feel the blood rush to her head. She balled her hands into fists and went after the girl. But the girl had tossed the magazine to a huge boy, who held it over his head, waving it triumphantly.

"Why don't you come get it, shorty?" he said with a

sneer, while stretching his arms up even higher into the clear, spring sky.

Liane looked around helplessly. Now what? The others, who had encircled her out of curiosity, looked away. Of course. What could she do against Marita and Robin? There probably wasn't a single person at her new school who wasn't afraid of the twins. Liana sighed. Why did her parents have to move to this horrible city anyway? But just as she was trying to figure out how to get her magazine back from Robin, a bell sounded. Recess was over!

"Alright then, matchstick," said Robin, waving the magazine under her nose again. "See you later."

"Give me my magazine back right now!" said Liane quietly.

Robin raised his eyebrows.

"Did you say something?"

"I said that you should give me my magazine back now," said Liane, a little louder this time.

Robin looked over at Marita.

"Did you understand what she just said?"

Marita just shrugged her shoulders.

"Give it up, Robin. It's enough. Let's give it back to her now. If a teacher comes, we'll be in serious trouble."

Robin shook his head.

"Are you kidding me? You really want me to quit, just when we started having fun? Come here, little matchstick, come get your magazine back!"

Liane was close to blowing up.

"Give me back my magazine right now!" she screamed at Robin, standing defiantly with her hands on her hips.

Robin laughed at her and then took a look at the page Liane had been reading.

"'Horseback riding camp in idyllic Upper Marlboro'... Oh you've got to be kidding me, you're not going to tell me that you're into riding horses, are you?" He sniffed the air loudly. "So we've got us a cowgirl. I should have known, considering how much it smells like a stable here."

Liane heard a few giggles and felt her face go red. Why couldn't Robin just leave her alone? Ever since he got caught smoking in the bathroom because of her, he hadn't missed an opportunity to get back at her. By coincidence, she had noticed the smell of smoke in the hallway and was afraid that something was on fire. After she alerted the hall monitor, Robin got caught and was given detention. It was the second time that semester and his parents must have been furious. She hadn't purposely told on him, but Liane understood why he was mad. Still, that didn't give him the right to be so mean to her! Robin's twin sister, Marita, probably wouldn't be so bad on her own, but she was totally under Robin's thumb and did whatever he told her to do, especially when he felt like picking on Liane.

Now what? She couldn't let them keep her magazine.

Liane took a deep breath, walked over to Robin and ripped the magazine out of his hand with a sharp jerk.

"Hey, what do you think you're doing?" he yelled and moved threateningly closer to her. "You just wait, you little red-haired toad. Now you're really in for it!"

Liane gaped at him breathlessly and tightened her grip on her magazine. Robin grabbed her arm so tightly that she wanted to scream. "I can easily take care of a little worm like you," he growled and ripped the magazine away from her. Robin was very big for his age and Liane didn't stand a chance against him. She watched helplessly as he waved the magazine under her nose.

"What's going on here?"

Liane turned around and looked right into the face of Vice Principal Dittmann. He looked sternly at her from underneath his bushy black eyebrows. He was well known for being tough with everyone who didn't follow his strict rules. Even Robin seemed to shrink into his shirt as he tried to slip away.

"Just a moment, young man."

Vice Principal Dittmann laid a hand on his shoulder and turned Robin around to face him. "First of all, I'd like to know what's going on here." He took the magazine out of Robin's hand and looked at the title. "Horse Review," he read out loud and looked at Liane. "Does this belong to you?" Liane's face got hot and then cold. If she said yes, Robin would be in deep trouble again. But if she said no, then she'd never get her magazine back and since she had already used up her allowance, she wouldn't be able to buy a new one. "I'm waiting for an answer," said Vice Principal Dittmann. He asked again impatiently, "Does it belong to you or not?"

"I... er, no, well I... er yes," stammered Liane as her face turned beet red.

"Well, which is it now? Yes or no?"

Vice Principal Dittmann appeared to be on the verge of losing his patience.

"Yes," whispered Liane, lowering her head.

"Well here you go then; now you have it back," said the educator. His gaze moved to Robin and then to Marita. "And our twins here took it away from you?"

"Er, no," Liane said quickly.

"Now I find that hard to believe after all the screaming and commotion I just heard," said Vice Principal Dittmann so authoritatively that Liane didn't dare to contradict him.

"Alright then, Robin and Marita Stoltz. Off to the principal's office. You already know the way."

"Oh please, not to the principal's office," whined Marita. "Our father said that if we get into trouble one more time at school, then Robin won't be allowed to go to camp in Italy with the soccer team. He's been looking forward to it for so long!"

"He should have thought about that earlier," said Vice Principal Dittmann impassively and shuffled the two of them along in front of him. When they passed Liane, Robin raised his head. "I'll get you back for that," he whispered and looked at her with his eyes glinting angrily.

Liane swallowed and watched him go, her hands shaking. Robin's threat sounded dead serious and she could only hope that his temper would cool off by the end of Spring break. Although deep down, she knew that Robin was one of those people who only left you alone after they'd had their revenge…

Liane slowly entered the school building and just managed to slip into her classroom ahead of her math teacher, Mrs. Hosiak. She sighed as she walked over to the empty desk in the last row where she sat all alone. At least Marita and Robin were two grades ahead of her. Seeing them every day in the schoolyard was bad enough. And she was glad that it was almost Spring break.

Liane stood her math book on her desk and put the pony magazine behind it so that Mrs. Hosiak couldn't see it.

Horseback riding camp in idyllic Marlboro… every guest will have a pony or horse to care for…

Her parents weren't exactly thrilled that she wanted to go away during Spring break. Their move had cost enough money already. And not just that.

"Wouldn't you rather do things during vacation with your new friends?" her mother asked.

Liane just said something unintelligible. Her parents had enough to do with their new jobs at the moment, so she didn't want to tell them about her problems in school.

Because neither of them got home before the evening, they hadn't noticed that Liane had never gone to a friend's house after school since their move to Washington, DC.

Liane looked out of the window and started to dream. Oh, to finally go riding again! In her mind's eye, she saw lush green meadows with lots of ponies and horses on them. She couldn't wait to spend a few peaceful, undisturbed days in the country!

Chapter 2

"What a mess!"

Marty slammed the front door behind her and stomped across the courtyard toward the open stable.

June looked up, surprised, and put the saddle soap and damp sponge down on the ground.

"What's wrong?"

Her mother brushed a wild lock of her red hair out of her face and groaned. "Farmer Myers just called. The Haflinger Gang …"

"… are in his field again," June completed her mother's sentence.

"Exactly," sighed Marty. "Somehow those rascals

managed to break out again." She thought for a minute and then gave June a sweet-as-sugar smile.

"Say, honey, would you mind riding over there to see if you can bring them back?"

"Me?"

June frowned.

"Why me? I was just cleaning Nelson's saddle. After all, we're going to be in a tournament next week." She looked sadly at her black saddle and could see that only half of it was clean, shining in the sunlight.

"But it doesn't make much sense to do all that now," Marty said airily. "It'll just be filthy again by next weekend."

"And would you mind telling me how I'm supposed to catch five horses and bring them back to our farm?" June asked darkly. She knew that her mother was right, but if she wouldn't be getting a new saddle, then she at least wanted the saddle she had to be in the best condition possible.

"Four," Marty corrected her. "You only have to catch four horses. Nano is still back there on the paddock."

She motioned with her head to the little chestnut with the light colored mane and tail. He stood in the shadow of an old lime tree, dozing with his eyes half shut.

"Now that he belongs to Charly, he doesn't go along with the others when they get into trouble. He'll sure be happy this afternoon when she gets here."

Of course! June had almost forgotten that the camp kids were arriving today. Her thoughts were so preoccupied with the tournament that she wasn't aware of anything else. That meant she had no choice but to round up the Haflingers on her own. Marty had more than enough to do before the guests arrived.

"All right, but can I at least use your saddle? The other half of mine isn't done yet."

"Sure," Marty beamed. "And you can take Modena, if you'd like."

June shook her head.

"No thanks. I'll take Nelson."

She was fond of her mother's Oldenburg mare, but given the choice June naturally preferred Nelson, her wonderful Anglo-Arabian. As always, her heart leapt when she approached the beautiful white horse with the big dark eyes that was out on the paddock. As soon as he saw her coming, he walked inquisitively in her direction, neighing quietly.

"Oh, Nelson."

June put her arms around his neck and rubbed her face in the gelding's silky-soft mane. Her horse didn't move a millimeter from the spot.

"Come on, we have to go round up the Haflinger Gang again. I don't have any idea how we'll do it, but we'll figure something out."

She attached the lead to Nelson's bridle and led him from the paddock. In a flash, he was brushed and saddled and June was riding him off the farm, holding the rein loosely. She had four ropes tied around her waist and she hoped that none of the Haflingers had thrown off his bridle.

The sun was shining, the birds were singing and the trees were showing the first flecks of green. In the distance she could see the mountains reaching high into the sky. The snow on the mountaintops looked like sugary icing. On any other day, June would've been elated to be riding out on her beloved white horse, but this time the feeling was outweighed by her disappointment that once again there would be no time for training. By the time she made it back to the farm with all of the Haflingers, the first camp guests would have arrived. And when the campers were there, Marty seldom had time to help her train. When June recently tried to talk to her about it, Marty hugged her and said, "I'm so sorry, June. I know how important the tournament is for you. But our guests have priority. You know how it is: the customer is king."

Just thinking about that made the corners of June's mouth lift into a grin. She still found it strange to hear her mother – of all people! – quoting sayings like that. But ever since the vacation camp business at Sunshine Farm had started up, Marty had even started acting like a real businesswoman. Sometimes. Her new business partner seemed to be a real miracle worker. Not only were they able to purchase five new, well-trained school horses, but all the buildings on their horseshoe-shaped courtyard were going to be renovated and enlarged, one after the

17

other. The reason for it all was the partner's daughter, Charly, who was a close friend of June's. She liked nothing better than to visit Sunshine Farm and go trotting through the fields on Nano, her Haflinger. At first Charly didn't even like horses. When June thought back to how withdrawn the dark-haired girl had been on her first visit, she could only shake her head.

Suddenly a shrill whinny interrupted her thoughts. She had been so deep in thought that she hadn't noticed that she had already reached Farmer Myers' fields. A powerful, small chestnut stood relatively close to her in the cornfield with his head held high, neighing.

Navajo!

He was the ringleader of the Haflinger Gang and as he saw her getting closer, he shook his head stubbornly before turning on his hind legs and galloping away. June's jaw dropped and she gaped as he ran over to the other three members of the Haflinger Gang who were at the other end of the field.

"Oh no," June mumbled. "How am I ever going to get them out of there?"

If only her friends Ben, Lena and Maxi were here. But today, of all days, they each had other plans and wouldn't get to Sunshine Farm until later. As if that weren't enough, June heard a tractor approaching. Amidst loud squeaking and rattling noises, the sinister-looking vehicle pulled up in front of her and a huge bald man with a fiery red face jumped off.

"For crying out loud! I am sick and tired of your lousy nags. Do you hear me?"

June would have loved to tell him that there was no way she could *not* hear him because he was yelling so loudly. But she decided to keep that thought to herself since Farmer Myers didn't have much of a sense of humor. Especially not when he was this angry. And whenever he saw June, he was usually pretty angry. Of course that was because the only time she went over to his fields was when the Haflingers had gotten loose again and were trampling his fields. June could even understand his anger a little. The Haflingers got loose pretty frequently. And Farmer Myers had the misfortune of having his fields border directly on Sunshine Farm.

"This time was once too often!" Farmer Myers screamed. "This time I'm calling the police. You can tell that to your mother. And now see to it that you get these miserable creatures out of my field."

He clumsily climbed back onto his tractor, revved the motor and drove back down the path he had just come up. June watched him for a while and then dismounted.

"Sorry about that, buddy, but if I ride through the field with you, he'll probably flip out completely."

June led Nelson to a nearby tree. How dumb that she hadn't thought of taking a bridle for her white horse. She thought for a moment, and then tied one of the ropes around his neck. Then she attached another rope to it and tied the other end to a strong tree branch. Not quite according to regulations, but it would do for now. With the two other lead ropes in her hand, June slowly walked toward the Haflingers on the narrow path that the farmer had left between his two fields. They had spread out on the field again and were watching her from under their thick, white forelocks. Nino stood closest to her so June approached him with her outstretched hand. Luckily she always had a few treats in her pocket. Nino stood there calmly and didn't bat an eyelash as she came closer. June fed him a treat while carefully attaching the lead rope to his bridle with her other hand. She let out a sigh of relief. That was much easier than she had expected it to be. With a little luck, the others might even follow her when she led Nino over to Nelson. But that was too optimistic. Navajo, Ninja and Noel weren't the slightest bit interested in Nino being led off. Instead they happily trotted in the other direction. June decided to tie Nino up next to Nelson and try her luck again with the others. But now she had a problem: she only had one rope. She had expected the others to follow once she led one of them away. But the members of the Haflinger Gang weren't so easily convinced. What could she do now?

June gave it some thought. Then she had an idea. Of course! She had to catch Navajo. He was the ringleader, so the others would follow him. Why hadn't she thought of that sooner?

She held the rope in her hand more tightly and approached Navajo with great determination. Of course he was farthest away from her. He didn't move from the spot and, alert, observed her as she carefully approached him.

"Come here little fella, I've got a treat for you," June cooed and tried not to let her anger color her voice.

Navajo stood still and looked at her as if he didn't have a care in the world. June held out a treat for him and he cautiously craned his neck toward it. Slowly June moved the hand that was holding the rope from behind her back. But just as she was about to fasten it to the snap hook on the chestnut's bridle, he quickly snatched the treat and galloped off to the other side of the field. He came to a stop there and looked at her quizzically. June sighed and walked in his direction. As soon as she got to within a few feet of him, he turned on his heels and galloped off. He played his little game four more times and just as she was ready to give up, he suddenly trotted over to Nino and Nelson and stayed with them. Ninja and Noel then joined him. When June reached them, panting and out of breath, the powerful chestnut patiently allowed her to attach the rope to his halter.

"That's just like you, isn't it," she scolded. "First you let me chase you all over the field and then you act like nothing happened. Well, we're lucky it didn't rain today. The ground is so dry that you couldn't do too much damage." She untied Nelson and attached the other ropes to Ninja and Noel's halters. "I just hope that you behave a little better when the campers are here."

Navajo shook his head and snorted. If June hadn't known it was impossible, she almost would have believed that he was laughing at her...

Chapter 3

"Well, here we are."

At the top of the hill, Liane's mother turned right into the driveway and came to a stop directly in front of the large residence. Before Liane could even open her car door, a woman walked out of the front door of the house and approached her, smiling. Liane could hardly believe her eyes. The woman's hair was the same fiery red color as her own. That had to be a good sign! At least no one here would dare to make jokes about her hair color. Liane pushed aside all her negative thoughts about school so that they wouldn't cloud her mood. She wasn't about to let it ruin her vacation, too.

"Hi, I'm Martha Sunshyne," said the woman as she walked over to Liane and her mother with her hand extended.

"I'm Mrs. Holler," said Liane's mother and shook her hand. "And this is my daughter, Liane."

"Welcome to Sunshine Farm, Liane." Marty smiled at her.

"Thank you, Mrs., er, Sunshyne."

"You can call me Marty. That's what everyone here calls me." Then Marty pointed to a smaller building next to the large farmhouse.

"That's where our camp guests live. You're the first one here today, Liane. That means that you have first choice of where you'd like to sleep."

"The first?"

Suddenly Liane had a funny feeling in her stomach. What would the other camp guests be like?

"How many are coming?"

"There'll be ten of you," Marty answered. "Actually, there'll be a total of 15 people."

"Fifteen?"

"Well, if you count my daughter June and her friends, then that makes 15 kids. And speak of the devil …" Marty took a deep breath and looked over at the car that was slowly pulling up the driveway. "That's Maxi and Lena over there. Now we're only missing Ben and Charly."

Two girls jumped out of the car and walked over to Marty.

"Liane, meet Maxi and Lena," Marty introduced the girls. "They board their horse Olaf here at our farm."

Their horse? Liane looked at the two girls, admiringly. Did that really mean that they had a horse of their very own?

"Hi Liane," Maxi and Lena said. "Have you ever ridden before?"

"Er, yes, a while ago," said Liane and added quietly, "before we moved."

"Really, you moved?" asked the girl who had been introduced as Maxi. "Where do you live now?"

"In the middle of Washington, DC. You can't ride there. Well, there are riding stables, but my parents say that it's much too expensive there."

"You poor thing," the other girl said sympathetically. "And where did you live before that?"

"In a small village out in the country," said Liane. "There was an open stable right around the corner from where we lived. And there was a horse there that I took care of. A Haflinger."

The thought of the little gelding named Star Money made Liane's heart feel heavy. But why were the girls looking at her so strangely and grinning so conspiratorially?

"Are you saying that you like Haflingers?"

Liane nodded slowly.

"Well, then you've come to the right place. We've got *five* Haflingers – well, actually just four because the fifth belongs to another girl."

"You have Haflingers?" Liane asked excitedly. "Where?"

The girls looked over toward the paddock next to the big stable. Liane could see a chestnut standing some distance away. Could that be one of the Haflingers? But what about the other four? She wasn't the only one wondering about that.

"Hey, Marty, where's the rest of the Haflinger Gang?"

Haflinger Gang? Liane couldn't figure out what they were talking about.

Marty, who had just been animatedly talking with Liane's mother, shrugged her shoulders and sighed.

"Oh, they ran off again. June's rounding them up right now." She paused a moment to think. "Say, do you feel like catching up with her? She's probably got her hands full with those rascals."

"Of course," Maxi called excitedly. "And we'll take Liane along with us. She likes Haflingers, you know."

"Oh really?" Marty laughed somewhat painfully. "How nice."

Liane looked to her mother for reassurance. She felt bad saying goodbye to her mother in such a rush, but on the other hand, she was excited about the Haflingers that Lena and Maxi had just told her about.

Mrs. Holler took her daughter in her arms and gave her a big hug.

"Go on, honey. Enjoy your vacation, okay?"

Liane nodded and swallowed. She wasn't going to start crying now, was she?

"Come on with us," said Lena and simply pulled

Liane along. "Let's hurry. June can use all the help she can get to bring back five horses."

"Five? I thought there were four," said Liane, confused.

"That's right, but wherever June is, Nelson is sure to go."

"Except in school," Lena laughed. "Can you imagine the look on her teacher's face if she showed up at school with her horse?"

Maxi and Lena got such a kick out of that thought that they didn't notice how grim Liane's expression turned when they mentioned the word "school."

School!

Just hearing the word gave her hives. Thank goodness it was vacation! She turned around to look at her mother and wave to her. No matter what she wasn't going to let anything ruin her fun this week!

"And you can pick out which of them you'd like to take care of," joked Maxi, after they had walked a bit.

"Can I really choose one myself?" Liane asked happily.

"Well, actually I meant that as a joke. I think that Marty decides who gets which horse based on how experienced everyone is. But if you've already had a pony to care for, then you're certainly not a beginner any more, are you?"

Liane thought about that for a minute.

"No, not really. Why do you ask?"

"Well, um, the Haflingers aren't especially well, um, trained... so they need an experienced rider. Luckily Marty was able to buy a few well-trained school horses with the money her new partner gave her; otherwise Sunshine Farm wouldn't really have gotten off the ground. I mean, just think how things would have turned out if Charly hadn't tried to run away in the middle of the night with Nano. I mean, it was even lucky that June broke her arm, even if that meant that she had to miss out on the tournament."

Run away in the middle of the night? Broken arm? Missing the tournament? Liane shook her head. This place sure sounded exciting! But before she could ask any questions, she noticed a strange creature ahead on the edge of the forest. It was big, wide and had – Liane couldn't believe her eyes – several heads.

"There they are now!" Lena called. "Come on, Liane. Now you'll get to meet June and the Haflingers."

Liane shook her head. A great big being with several heads. That was just crazy! But then she realized that what she was seeing was a girl who was leading two horses on one hand and three on the other and it was taking all her strength and concentration to keep any of them from breaking loose.

"Maxi! Lena!" the girl with the medium-blonde hair shouted, obviously relieved. "Thank goodness you're here. If I had to do this any longer my arms would have fallen off."

Suddenly she noticed Liane and gave Maxi a questioning look.

"This is Liane," said Maxi. "She's one of the camp guests. We took her with us because, believe it or not, she likes Haflingers."

"Really?"

The girl looked at Liane, unsure of what to think.

"Well, if it were up to me, they would be a little more sensitive." She threw a loving glance in the direction of her elegant white horse. "Like Nelson, for instance."

"Pay no attention to her," Lena laughed. "If it were up to June, all horses would be exactly like Nelson. And imagine how boring that would be."

"Hmm." After Maxi took the lead for Noel and Ninja, June rubbed her right shoulder. "I don't mind a little boredom now and then. That sure would be a lot better than constantly chasing after these rascals to get them out of Farmer Myers' fields. You wouldn't believe how angry he was this time. I think he might call the police."

"Oh I wouldn't worry. Charly's dad will deal with it. Besides, the Haflingers are probably insured for that."

"I sure hope so. But with all the chaos in my mother's office, I wouldn't be surprised if she forgot to make the payments."

"Oh, I'm sure that's something else Charly's dad takes care of," Lena said confidently and grabbed two of the chestnuts.

"And Liane? Have you chosen one already?"

31

Liane leaned her head to the side and carefully looked over each of the four Haflingers. They were all sweet and she didn't know which of them she liked best. The one with the narrow blaze and the really long mane maybe? Or the one with the pretty spot on his forehead? Or maybe the big one that didn't have any markings? No.

One look at the powerful chestnut with the mischievous expression and Liane knew which one she like best. She walked over to him and with her fingers, she gently stroked the white stripe over his nostrils. The other girls broke out into loud laughter and she turned around to look at them in astonishment.

"What is up with you?"

"Oh, just that you picked yourself the right horse," Maxi giggled. "That's Navajo, the biggest troublemaker of them all."

"Troublemaker?" Liane took a good look at Navajo. "What's that supposed to mean?"

"That he's the one who's always coming up with new pranks," Lena explained. "He's the ringleader of the Haflinger Gang, and when it gets too boring for him he comes up with all kinds of crazy ideas."

"And that can get pretty exhausting for us," June groaned. "I'm dead tired now. I'll just have to forget about training for the tournament today, even though it's only a week away. I'm going to make a fool of myself in front of all of those people."

"Of course you won't make a fool of yourself," Maxi

tried to console her. As far as she was concerned, there was a solution for every problem. "Tomorrow we'll first help you with your work and then we'll set up some obstacles on the jumping field. Liane will help, too. Won't you, Liane?"

Liane, who had only been listening with half an ear, nodded absently. She only had eyes for Navajo, who was giving her a bemused look from underneath his thick forelock and snorting. As far as she was concerned, he was the most beautiful horse she had ever seen.

Chapter 4

"Wow, there's a lot going on over there," Lena called out as she reached the top of the hill. From that vantage point she had a view of the entire Sunshine Farm.

"It looks like everyone has arrived."

"Well let's get going," said June and marched off purposefully with Nelson. "My mother is sure to need help."

The three girls followed her and before long they were back at Sunshine Farm. It seemed more like they had landed in the middle of a busy beehive, and June had trouble finding her mother, who was standing in the center of a group of people, explaining to them where to stow their gear.

"Ah, June, I'm glad you're back," she called out in relief when she caught sight of her daughter. "Did you, er, bring them all back? Then could you be an angel and show, er, Martin and his sister Janine where the bedrooms are?"

"I'll do it right away, but first I have to take Nelson to the paddock."

June led her horse to the hitching post and quickly took off his saddle and snaffle bit before leading him to the field behind the house. She quickly gave him a treat and a friendly clap on his gleaming backside before closing the paddock gate behind him. Then she went back to the boy and girl who were waiting for her.

"Hi, I'm June. And you're Martin and Janine, right?"

"You got that right," said the boy, who smiled as he reached out his hand to her. June liked him immediately, with his dark blonde curls and friendly smile.

"Do you live here all the time?" Janine asked and looked at her admiringly. "That must be totally cool."

June nodded.

"Yeah, it is. Come on, I'll take you to the dairy kitchen."

"The dairy kitchen?"

Martin gaped at her with his mouth open.

"What in the world is that?"

"Don't worry," June laughed. "That's just what the building was called when this used to be a working farm with cows and everything. That was a long time ago, but for some reason, the name just stuck. Come with me."

June led Janine and Martin to the smaller building next to the house where she lived with her mother.

There was a lot of commotion in the dairy kitchen because in the meantime, all of the guests had arrived, each looking to lay claim to a bed. June came to a stop in the first room.

"This is the bedroom for the girls," she said to Janine. "Pick out a bed and unpack your stuff."

Then she walked with Martin to the back room, which was slightly smaller.

"And this is where the boys sleep."

"Am I the only boy?" Martin asked and looked around self-consciously.

"Hmm." June shrugged her shoulders. "To be honest, I have no idea. Maybe someone else is still coming."

She looked around the front room and counted the girls who were chatting and giggling as they unpacked their things.

"… eight, nine."

She turned around to Martin.

"Counting you that makes ten. I'm sorry, but it looks like you really are the only boy. Does it bother you to sleep here alone?"

Martin thought for a minute.

"Well, I wouldn't mind having a little company, but I guess I'll survive. At least I've got plenty of time to pick out which bed I want."

He tossed his duffle bag onto the bed that was to the

right of the door and then climbed up the ladder. "It's not bad up here. I think this is where I'll sleep. But later if I decide I don't like it, I'll just switch to another bed."

That's what I call positive thinking," laughed June. "Maybe we can ask Ben to spend a couple of nights here with you."

"Ben? Who's that?"

"A friend. He'll be here any minute now, then I can introduce you."

Martin hung his head out of the bed and looked deep into her eyes.

"Can I ask you something? This Ben, is he, well, I mean, is he your boyfriend?"

Now it was June's turn to look at him with wide-open eyes.

"What do you mean by that, my boyfriend?"

"You know, your boy-friend," Martin sighed. "Not just a friend, but a boyfriend." He looked at June helplessly. "Do you understand what I mean?"

June nodded slowly. She suddenly felt hot and hoped that Martin couldn't see from up there how red her face was now.

"I, um, think so. Well, Ben is a friend, but not my boyfriend. Um, I mean he's my friend, but …"

"Okay, okay," Martin calmed her down and then jumped down to the floor. "I understand. This Ben is a good friend of yours. That's great. If that's the case, then I don't have a problem with him sleeping in here with me for a few days."

"Yes, er, okay then …"

June stood in the door feeling a little uncertain. She twisted a few strands of hair around her finger.

"Well, I guess I'll be going then. We'll be seeing, um, each other a little later."

She turned on her heel and walked out to the courtyard as quickly as possible. Then she leaned against the side of the house, closed her eyes and took a deep breath. A friend, my friend, my boyfriend. This guy, Martin, had her totally confused. But he was really nice, with his mischievous smile and funny curls…

"Hey June, are you already out of steam? The week just got started."

June opened her eyes and needed a moment to adjust to the bright light of the midday sun. Marty was standing in front of her, impatiently swinging a bridle in one hand.

"Please take a look to see if our guests have unpacked their things. If so, we can meet up in the courtyard and I'll tell them who gets which horse. After that we'll go to the arena."

"Okay."

June pushed herself off the wall with her palms and went back to the dairy kitchen. As she entered the room, the girls stopped talking and looked at her, smiling with anticipation.

"My mother said that we should all meet up in the courtyard once you've finished unpacking. She'll let you know which horse you get and then we'll saddle up."

"Well, finally," a tall, slender girl with straight black hair murmured as she stood up. "I was starting to think we'd be stuck in this shack forever."

June was speechless and stared at her as she walked out of the room.

"Pay no attention," Liane consoled her. "Chantal seems to think she's the center of the universe. At least, that was my impression of her. What do you others think?"

She turned around to the other girls who giggled and nodded in response. June swallowed. She was going to have to get used to the fact that there would always be a few difficult guests at Sunshine Farm. Fortunately most of the campers were really nice and easy to get along with – like Liane, whom she liked from the moment they were introduced.

"Alright, let's get going," she said and made a face. "We don't want to keep Madame waiting any longer."

As the other girls stormed past her, she pulled Janine aside.

"Hey Janine, er, could you ask your brother to come, too? I'll go on ahead with the others and we'll meet on the bench under the big chestnut tree."

Janine ran off and June breathed a sigh of relief. Whew. It was probably better if she and Martin didn't meet up any more when they were alone. Somehow he had her totally confused.

"Hey there," Liane interrupted her thoughts. "Do you think your mother will let me ride Navajo?"

June laughed.

"I have no idea. Maybe you should just ask her. But if I were you, I'd think that over again carefully."

"Why do you say that?"

Liane wrinkled her forehead.

"Well, we told you that Navajo has nothing but foolishness in his head. Sometimes he can be pretty sassy."

"Oh that doesn't matter. I'm used to that already from Star Money. He's a Haflinger, too."

"Star Money? Is that your horse?"

"No." Suddenly Liane looked sad. "I took care of him. But then we moved to DC and I haven't seen him since."

June put her hand on Liane's shoulder to comfort her.

"I'm really sorry to hear that. You know what? I'll talk to my mother. If you've already taken care of a horse, then that makes you one of our experienced riders, which means that you'd be allowed to ride Navajo."

"Would you really do that for me?" Liane looked at her gratefully. "That would be great."

"Sure!"

June looked around the courtyard.

"I'll go look for her right now."

Before long she found Marty in the tack room and told her about her conversation with Liane.

"Do you really think so? I thought we'd give Navajo to Chantal. She seems to be the most experienced rider."

June thought back to earlier in the afternoon and how

Navajo had her chasing him all over Farmer Myers' fields. It would be the perfect punishment for the naughty chestnut to be stuck with arrogant Chantal riding him. But on the other hand, she had made a promise to Liane.

"Liane already had a Haflinger to care for and besides, you don't really know that Chantal is such an experienced rider. Maybe she bragged on her registration form."

Marty's lips twitched.

"You may be right. At any rate, she certainly is pretty pleased with herself. Okay then, Liane will get Navajo and Chantal will have Prince Pepper."

"I'm sure she'll like that," June mumbled. The elegant nine-year-old Hanoverian gelding was one of the new school horses that Marty had bought for the camp. The brown horse was very well trained and looked like a dream, too. Marty felt that he was almost too good to be a school horse and only gave him to experienced children to ride. Actually June was annoyed that she accidentally did Chantal such a big favor, but it was important to her that Liane get Navajo. As she started to walk over to her new friend to tell her the good news, a big dark car pulled up in the driveway, coming to a stop in front of the house. The doors opened and a tall man and a dark-haired girl got out.

"Charly! Well, it's about time!"

June ran over to her friend and gave her a big hug.

"I'm so glad you're finally here!"

"I could hardly wait, too," said Charly and let go of her. "Where's Nano? I missed him so much!"

"He's over there on the paddock. Come on, let's go right over to him."

She hooked her arm through Charly's and together they walked up to the paddock where the Haflingers were grazing peacefully. Seeing them like this, it was hard to believe that just a few hours ago they were making all sorts of trouble off the farm. June looked at them suspiciously. Who could guess what they'd come up with this week…?

Chapter 5

"Okay, let's get started now."

Marty sat down casually at the wooden table under the big chestnut tree and smiled at the group.

"I'll bet you'd all like to know which horses I've picked out for you."

Liane balled her hands into fists and took a deep breath. Did June keep her promise? She'd find out soon enough.

"Martin? You get Modena. She's the cute black mare over there on the paddock. Take good care of her – Modena is my horse."

"Okey dokey," said Martin, smiling broadly. "At our stable back home they call me the horse whisperer."

"Well, then I feel much better now," laughed Marty, who seemed to take to Martin's congenial manner immediately. "Lucy, you get Flori. That's the little black pony that you may have already seen. We have him for our youngest guests."

"How sweet," Lucy squealed and clapped her hands together happily.

Liane figured that the little girl with the straight blonde hair was at most eight or nine years old, much younger than the other campers. But that didn't seem to bother her in the least. Liane sighed. It was so unfair that some people could be bursting with self-confidence while others – like herself – hardly had any at all.

Marty continued distributing the horses. Antonia, who wanted everyone to call her Toni, got a little chestnut mare called Miss Dignified. Alina, the girl with the brown curls, got a pony mare named Doreen. Connie, the cheeky girl, got a huge brown horse named Welcome. And Chantal got the lovely gelding called Prince Pepper. Liane couldn't help it, but for some reason, she didn't particularly like Chantal. She acted like she owned the whole world. But that wasn't her problem. She promised herself that she would just do her best to avoid Chantal all week long and not let her ruin her vacation!

"So, now things will get especially exciting," Marty said, laughing. "Now we're up to the Haflinger Gang."

"Haflinger Gang," Martin laughed. "What's that all about?"

"Well, our Haflingers are still a bit – how shall I put it? – boisterous. Which is why they will only be ridden by more advanced riders." Marty sighed audibly and looked at her slip of paper. "Janine, you get Noel, and Vicky, you get Ninja."

Liane held her breath. That left Laura and her and Navajo was still up for grabs!

"Laura, you get Navajo. And Liane will be taking Nino."

Liane's jaw dropped. She could feel her eyes filling with tears. She bit her lower lip – just don't cry!

"Are you okay?" Toni whispered to her. "Are you not feeling well?"

Liane shook her head and cleared her throat. "No, thanks, really, I'm okay," she croaked in a hoarse voice while turning her head away quickly. It would have been too embarrassing if she had broken down in tears here in front of everybody.

"Okay, then you can go to your horses now. Charly and I will help you so that you know which horse is which."

As if she were in a trance, Liane followed Vicky, Laura and Janine to the Haflinger paddock. The chestnuts stood with their heads held high and eyed them with curiosity. It broke her heart to see Laura walk over to Navajo with the lead rope in her hand. Maybe she had written about her riding experience in more detail on her application form? Did Marty figure Liane wasn't good enough to ride the leader of the Haflinger Gang? She swallowed and went over to Nino, who looked out at her from under his blond forelock with a friendly expression.

"It's not your fault," she said quietly and gently stroked his light colored velvety soft nose. She attached the rope to his bridle and walked behind the others to lead him off the paddock.

"Hey Liane! Can I introduce you to my friend Charly?"

Liane looked up when she recognized June's voice and looked into the face of a girl with dark hair.

"Charly was once a camper here, until her father became part owner of Sunshine Farm and bought Nano for her. Nano's the smallest of the Haflingers."

Liane looked at Charly with a mixture of jealousy and admiration. Some people got all the luck!

"Hey wait a minute." June looked at Nino, surprised. "That's not Navajo. Did you pick the wrong horse?"

Liane shook her head.

"No, why? Your mother said that I'd be riding Nino."

"Really? That surprises me. Because I told her that she should give you Navajo and she didn't have a problem with that. Are you totally sure that you didn't misunderstand her?"

"Totally sure," said Liane darkly. "Because in that case Laura would have misunderstood her, too. She's the one who got Navajo."

Liane motioned with her head toward the hitching post, where Laura was tying Navajo's lead.

"I'm sorry to hear that," said June sympathetically. "But you know what, I'll talk to my mother again this evening. I'm sure you don't mind riding Nino just this afternoon, huh? Right now my mother is so stressed that it's better if I don't try to talk to her."

Liane's heart leapt. Maybe June would still be able to change her mother's mind so that she would get Navajo after all. And until that happened, she'd take care of Nino.

"No problem. I think Nino's nice, too. After all, he's a Haflinger. And Haflingers are my favorite breed."

June made a face. "Another lunatic."

Charly giggled.

"Just ignore her. June just doesn't get it. She likes those nervous Thoroughbreds that want to run away from the slightest thing – sheesh." She shook her dark hair. "What a load of trouble."

"Nelson is not the slightest bit nervous," June grumbled, taking offense immediately. "And he doesn't run away from every little thing – he just enjoys galloping."

"Oh come on, get over yourself." Charly put her arm around her shoulder. "You don't mean to tell us that you don't have a sense of humor? After all, don't dish it out ..."

"... if you can't take it," June finished the sentence with a laugh. "Okay, okay, I get it already. But now I have to get going. I promised my mother that I would lunge little Lucy on Flori."

"And I have to get Nano down from the paddock," said Charly. "See you later, Liane."

"See you later." Liane watched Charly for a moment, and then she led Nino to the hitching post and tied him up between Navajo and Chantal's Prince Pepper.

"Don't come too close to me with that shaggy beast of yours," hissed Chantal. "Ponies like that tend to kick."

"Nino isn't a pony. He's a Haflinger," said Liane irritably and grabbed a currycomb out of the box of grooming supplies that stood in front of the hitching post. "And even if he were a pony, that doesn't mean he kicks. Besides, there are plenty of big horses that kick."

"Whatever."

Chantal gave her an arrogant smile and stroked Prince Pepper's chestnut coat that shone like gold in the sun. He truly was a beautiful horse and Liane had to admit that slender Chantal, with her shiny black hair, looked good with him.

She sighed and began currying. Although she would have preferred Navajo to Nino, and the boxy chestnut with the strong legs was more or less the exact opposite of sleek Prince Pepper, that didn't mean she was going to let anyone ruin her good mood. Chantal should just see how beautiful the Haflinger was about to look!

When she finished, she stepped back and admired her work. Now Nino's coat also shone like gold and his think blonde mane cascaded down his strong neck. She risked a sideways look at Laura and Navajo. The self confident Haflinger stood there with his head held high and looked mischievously out at the group. Would June be able to convince her mother to let her ride him after all? That would be too wonderful! Somehow she and that gelding with the challenging look in his eyes were on the same wavelength. But then she had a sudden pang of bad conscience as Nino gave her an affectionate look from under his forelock and she went over to him and gently scratched him behind his ears.

"And you're simply wonderful, too," she assured him and lay her head against his neck. "After all, you're a Haflinger and those are the greatest horses in the world!" Nino snorted and gently nudged her side, as if he were trying to underscore what she had just said. Liane laughed and went into the tack room to get his bridle. She tried to hurry because the others were nearly done saddling up their horses. As she approached Nino with the saddle and snaffle bit, she saw June with little Lucy and the funny black pony whose mane stood up in all directions crossing the courtyard. Chantal had also mounted her horse and was riding toward the arena on Prince Pepper. Liane watched them for a moment. They really did look excellent together. Chantal looked as if she already had spent an eternity in the saddle. Liane didn't have anything against her – but if only she weren't so arrogant!

She quickly saddled and snaffled Nino, led him a few steps and then climbed into the saddle. What a fantastic feeling to finally be sitting on a horse again! Walking to the riding arena on the back of the Haflinger had her feeling like she was floating on cloud nine.

"That one doesn't look bad on you either!" June called to her. She was standing in the middle of the arena, walking Flori on the lunge line. "It's easy to see that you've got a lot of riding experience."

Liane smiled at her gratefully. A little praise always felt good, especially since she wasn't sure how much she had forgotten since the last time she had ridden.

After all of them had walked for a while, Marty came to the arena and divided them into two groups. Liane was in the second group with Martin, Laura, Vicky and Chantal. Marty told them that they could break in their horses alone while she worked with the first group. Nino snorted happily and trotted off as soon as Liane took up the reins and gently urged him on. She wanted to sing out with joy because it felt so good!

Chapter 6

Lucy smiled brightly as she sat on the Shetland pony's broad back and stretched her arms up into the air.

"Now take your feet out of the stirrups and let your legs hang down," said June. "Just pretend that you're a tree."

"A tree?" asked Lucy, her eyes wide open. "Why should I do that?"

"You'll understand in a minute. Just pretend your arms are the branches that stretch up into the sky. Way up into the sky. And your legs are the roots that reach deep into the ground. Now close your eyes while you do it."

June observed with satisfaction how the little girl

stretched upwards and downwards before lithely sitting upright in the saddle again. She had learned from Marty that small children did better when you gave them an image to follow instead of constantly barking out "heels down!" or "shoulders back!" to them. And not just the small children. June herself often conjured up the picture of the tree in her mind's eye in order to sit up straight on the horse's back.

"You're doing great," she praised Lucy. "Now you can open your eyes again and hold on to the saddle strap. We're going to start trotting. Have you ever trotted before?"

Lucy nodded so emphatically that the black riding helmet on her head bobbed and wobbled.

June wasn't surprised, because it was clear from the way she sat on Flori that this wasn't the first time she had gone riding. At first the blonde girl had some trouble with posting, but once she became accustomed to the Shetland pony's fast steps, she improved quickly. While Lucy trotted joyfully back and forth, occasionally letting go with alternate hands, June curiously looked over the other riders.

Her gaze fell upon Martin first. He had taken up the reins with Modena and begun trotting. He appeared to be a little uncertain, but was taking care not to bounce too hard on the black mare's back and not to pull at her mouth with the bit. When he noticed her looking at him, he smiled and winked at her. June turned bright red and quickly looked in another direction. On the other side of

Luci on Flori

Juli

Martin on Modena

Chantal on Prince Pepper

Liane on Nino

the arena, Chantal trotted past with Prince Pepper. She sat up straight in the saddle, but June secretly saw quite a bit to criticize. Chantal was the kind of rider who never let the horse get warmed up first. She took up the reins almost immediately and held them rigidly. Prince Pepper held his head down, but gave off an impression of feeling cramped.

"You've got to give him more rein," Marty called to her. "Otherwise he'll push his back away and won't step down right in back."

June sighed with relief. Although Marty could be pretty disorganized, you could rely on her one thousand percent when it came to the well-being of the horses. Then she noticed Liane on Nino. She absolutely had to ask her mother why she didn't give her Navajo after all. Then again, the longer she watched, the more it seemed that that Haflinger and the girl with the short red hair seemed to fit together. Nino trotted contentedly and gave out a relaxed snort every few feet. When he tried to slow down here and there, Liane reacted immediately and urged him on again. June smiled. Liane really did seem to know how to handle Haflingers. She and Charly would surely have a lot to talk about because her friend was one of the biggest Haflinger fans that June had ever met. It was just amazing how the little chestnut and her friend had changed each other in such a short time. June could still remember how cranky and unsure Charly was the first time she came to Sunshine Farm. Seeing her now on

Nano, it was hard to believe that Charly was once afraid of horses!

June turned her attention back to Flori, who had taken advantage of her inattentiveness and slowed down to a walk. Lucy tried to urge him on with her short legs, but she didn't stand a chance with the stubborn pony that only shook his head. "Typical Flori," June laughed and touched his powerful backside with the long lunge crop. "As soon as you turn away, he does exactly what he wants to do. Now we'll trot from the left and then we'll change hands. Otherwise Flori will get dizzy."

"Not just Flori," Lucy giggled. "I'm getting dizzy myself."

After she trotted a few more rounds, June slowed Flori back down to a walk and hooked the lunge line onto the right bridle ring.

"You did really well," she said to Lucy. "I'll bet that by the end of the week you'll be riding by yourself."

"Do you really mean that?" asked Lucy and sat up even straighter. "That would be super!"

"Don't you worry," June assured her. "I know you'll be ready."

June could tell that all that praise made Lucy happy, because she seemed to grow a few inches taller in the saddle. If only all the riding students were as easy to handle as Lucy!

"But my riding teacher back home said that I should counter by holding up front," she heard Chantal whining.

"Whatever you hold up front you have to be able to drive from the back," retorted Marty. Oh my! Marty sounded as if she was really annoyed. "And when the horse yields, then you also have to yield – and not pull back all the time."

"When the horse is so tight mouthed, then I have to pull back. Back home we have much better school horses than here."

June's chin dropped. Prince Pepper – tight mouthed? She had ridden the beautiful chestnut herself and knew that he was very receptive to commands. What would Marty say to that?

She stared at Chantal as though she hadn't understood her. Then she opened her mouth, only to close it again. She took a deep breath and turned to Connie who was just trotting a circle on powerful Welcome.

June knew exactly what was going on in her mother's head. She was furious, which was why she was keeping her mouth shut. Because if she said something now, she would probably explode with anger. And, as she had taken to saying lately, the customer is king. June looked at Chantal doubtfully. But was that a rule that you always had to follow?

Nevertheless, the riding lesson continued without any further problems. Navajo periodically tried to run in a different direction than the one his rider wanted, but Laura was reasonably successful in keeping him under control. And when she needed help, Marty was there to chase him into the right direction.

Except for Chantal, everyone was in excellent spirits as they unsaddled the horses. June first took care of Lucy and Flori and then, once the round Shetland pony was back on the paddock, she looked around to see if anyone else needed her help.

"Hey June, could you hold Modena a minute? I can't find her lead." Martin had leaned his head to the side and looked at her with his blue eyes. June swallowed and took the reins. As if by chance, Martin's fingers brushed against hers and again she got that strange feeling in her belly.

"I'll be right back," Martin smiled and dashed off.

June stood there motionlessly and took a deep breath.

"What's eating you?"

As if by magic, Ben was suddenly standing in front of her.

"You look like you just saw a ghost. Are you okay?"

"What? Oh no… I mean, of course… er, yes."

Ben looked at her with wide-open eyes.

"What?"

"I, er, I mean, that I didn't see a ghost, so no. And yes, I am okay."

June wished she could just disappear; the whole situation was so embarrassing. Her best friend was looking at her like she was losing her marbles.

"Here, I found it."

Martin squeezed in between Modena and Doreen's backsides and swung the blue and white rope around with his hand. When he saw Ben, he stopped suddenly and gave him a quizzical look.

"This, er, this is …"

"I'm Ben," Ben interrupted June's stuttering and reached out to shake hands with Martin. "It's nice to meet you."

Martin sized him up from head to toe and then took his hand.

"My name is Martin. Are you June's, um, what did she say… buddy?"

Ben wrinkled his forehead. He looked over at June, who stood there helplessly, twirling a few strands of hair around her finger. Suddenly, Ben's forehead went smooth again and he began to smile understandingly.

"Oh yes, that's right. Buddy. I'm June's buddy. Isn't that right, June?"

June nodded weakly.

Martin smiled with relief and patted Ben on the back in a friendly way.

"June told me that there was another guy at the farm. Otherwise I'm the only one around. Do you feel like sleeping in my room sometime?"

Ben nodded.

"Sure, why not? I sleep here a lot during vacation. I might as well move in with you in the dairy kitchen."

"It's a deal then. How about getting started tonight? Then you can tell me all about the farm. And, of course, about June. How long have you two known each other?"

Martin put his arm on Ben's shoulder and led him a few steps away so that June couldn't hear what they were saying. What did he mean by that – telling him all about the farm and about June?

Absentmindedly, June walked across the courtyard toward her house. The others would do fine without her. She needed to be by herself for a few minutes.

But she didn't have a chance because as soon as she opened the front door, she ran into Marty, who was dashing down the stairs.

"June, thank goodness it's you. You and Mrs. Morris, you'll have to take care of everything for a while. I have to go over to Farmer Myers'."

"To Farmer Myers'?"

"He just called. And he's furious because the Haflingers destroyed his entire field. I have a feeling that he really will sue us if I don't find some way to appease him. Keep your fingers crossed for me, or it will be very expensive for us."

"Aren't we insured against something like that?"

"I don't think that the insurance company will be willing to pay if our horses are constantly running away. They probably call that breaching our duty of supervision or something like that." Marty slipped into her light brown loafers and, before June could say anything, was out the door.

Chapter 7

Oh no! June pulled off her steel-toed boots and went upstairs into the kitchen where Lena and Maxi's mother was already setting the table.

"Oh June, I'm glad you're here. Please put out the glasses. I have to check on the casserole so that it doesn't burn."

Cheryl Morris rushed to the oven and pulled open the door. A delicious smell streamed out into the room.

"Mmmm, a noodle casserole – how yummy!"

June's stomach suddenly started to growl loudly. It occurred to her that she hadn't eaten a thing in ages. Cheryl took two big steaming casserole dishes out and put them on the table.

"I hope it will be enough," she said. "I still have to get used to cooking for so many people."

June nodded. Thanks to Mr. Schultz's help, they now had more than twice as many horses as before and a corresponding number of campers. June still had to get used to having so many guests at the farm. Could it be that Marty had bitten off more than she could chew? And now there was trouble with Farmer Myers – because the Haflingers had torn up his entire field. June set the last glass down on the table and paused for a moment. What had Marty just said? The entire field had been destroyed? How strange. It certainly hadn't looked like the Haflingers had destroyed so much when she had retrieved them, especially with the ground so dry. Really, she would have noticed something like that, wouldn't she? June shrugged her shoulders. Farmer Myers was probably over-exaggerating again to scare Marty.

Besides, she had a lot of other things on her mind. The tournament, for instance. If she could convince someone to get up really early with her, then she might have enough time to get in a round of training with Nelson before the first riding lesson.

Maxi, Lena and Charly were all for the idea when June asked them about it over dinner.

"Of course we'll get up with you," said Charly. "It's the least I can do to help after ruining your last tournament."

"How did you ruin it?" asked Martin, who was sitting across from them with Ben.

61

"Oh," said Ben. "That's a very long story. If you're interested, I'll tell you tonight when we're in bed."

"Fine with me," said Martin, smiling at June from across the table. "As long as June's in the story, you can tell me anything."

June nearly choked on her noodles and coughed so loudly that Charly had to clap her on the back.

"Are you okay?" asked Charly.

June cleared her throat and took a big sip of water.

"Er, yes, thanks. Um, how do you all feel about playing a round of Trouble tonight?"

"Trouble?" Chantal asked across the table. "How boring. The only person I still play that with is my grandmother. Don't you have any more exciting games?"

June's chin dropped. Before she could say anything, Martin jumped to her defense.

"I don't know what your problem is. I think Trouble is lots of fun."

"Exactly," said Ben. "We had a really big tournament going with the last group of campers and had a great time. So, are you guys interested?"

Everyone nodded and Chantal finally agreed to join in.

"All right then, I suppose I don't have any other choice," she groaned and tossed her hair back affectedly. "To be honest, I thought camp would be a lot more exciting."

June balled her hands into fists. Who did this Chantal think she was? She would love to tell her to just leave if she didn't like it. But that was impossible because – how did Marty put it? The customer is king. Still, did that mean that you had to put up with everything?

"Pay no attention," Lena whispered. "We only have to put up with her for a week and then she'll be gone."

June nodded. Lena was right. She'd manage the one week with Chantal, especially since all the other campers seemed so nice. She especially liked Liane. But why didn't Marty give her Navajo? She'd have to ask her when she got back.

While June, Maxi and Lena cleared the table, Ben was already outside, setting up the Trouble tournament under the big chestnut tree in the middle of the courtyard. By the time the three of them got downstairs, Ben had already divided up the players. The tournament began with Chantal against Toni. It seemed to June that Chantal was pretty competitive for someone who didn't even want to play in the first place. In the end she won, but just barely, making it to the next round. June, on the other hand, lost to Janine and was out in the first round, making it easier for her to follow the action. In the end it was down to a battle between Chantal and Martin. June rooted for him and cheered loudly when he knocked out one of Chantal's pieces. But his luck didn't last for long because Chantal suddenly started rolling nothing but sixes, taking giant leaps to home base. Martin came close to catching up, but then she brought the last of her pieces home, winning the tournament.

"Darn it," June whispered to Charly. "Why did she have to win?"

"Who cares?" Charly looked at her innocently. "Would you rather have seen Martin win?"

"Er, not really," June stammered. "I mean, um... let's just say I would rather have seen Chantal lose."

"Got it," said Charly, smiling meaningfully. But June didn't have any time to think about Charly's odd comments, because at that moment, Marty pulled up the driveway in her old station wagon. She quickly ran over to her mother.

"So what did Farmer Myers say?"

Marty got out and slammed the door behind her.

"Good grief. I've never seen him that angry. And no small wonder, considering how his field looked."

"What do you mean, 'no small wonder, considering how his field looked'?" June repeated with surprise. Could it be that Farmer Myers wasn't exaggerating after all? "It didn't look so bad to me."

"Not so bad?" Marty raised her eyebrows. "There were places where everything had been trampled flat. You should have told me that the Haflingers destroyed everything!"

"But that's just it: they didn't!" exclaimed June. "I remember exactly what I thought to myself at the time – that it was lucky that the earth was so dry, because it prevented them from doing more damage."

"Whether the earth was dry or not, their little adventure will cost us a pile of money," groaned Marty and ran her fingers through her unruly red hair. "Sometimes I ask myself why we don't just sell the Haflingers."

"No way!"

Although the Haflingers had driven June crazy many times, by now she had grown so accustomed to them, that she couldn't imagine not having those mischievous chestnuts around.

"But you can't do that. Do I have to remind you that without them, there wouldn't be any Sunshine Farm?"

"And with them, there probably won't be for much longer, either," sighed Marty. "I have to call Michael and tell him what happened."

June breathed a sigh of relief. She was so happy that Charly's father had decided to become an investor in Sunshine Farm and that she and Marty didn't have to deal with Farmer Myers on their own. Mr. Schultz would know what to do. After all, it would be a huge joke if a successful financial advisor like him couldn't handle a stubborn farmer. Wouldn't it…?

Suddenly she remembered something.

"Wait a second!" she called and followed Marty.

"What now?"

"I was wondering, why didn't you give Navajo to Liane after all?"

"Liane?"

"You know, the girl with the red hair."

Marty looked at her as if she had no idea what she was talking about. Her visit with Farmer Myers must have really upset her. June could sympathize.

"You promised me that she would get Navajo."

"Okay, and didn't she?"

Sometimes she drives me up the wall, thought June.

"No, she didn't. She's riding Nino now."

"Yes, that's right. Nino. You said that the girl with the red hair wanted to ride Nino. So she's riding Nino."

"Not Nino," June said as gently as if she were speaking with a little child.

"Navajo. I said Navajo. You got it all confused."

"Oh my," Marty looked at her sadly. "I'm really sorry about that. Is she very sad?"

"I have no idea. We could tell her that it was a mistake and that she can trade. As long as that's okay with Laura."

"Laura?"

Marty wrinkled her forehead.

"The girl who's now riding Navajo."

"Oh. Hmm. I understand. Say June, do you think you could take care of that? I really don't have time for this sort of thing right now. I have to call Michael immediately," said Marty, beginning to sound a bit annoyed.

"Alright alright," June raised her hands as if to protect herself. "I'll take care of it. I just didn't want to overstep. It could had been that you did it for a reason."

"A reason?"

Marty laughed hysterically.

"I've got so much on my mind that I can't even think straight."

She put her arm around June's shoulder.

"No really, honey, I would be grateful to you if you could take care of it."

"Okay. Then you go call Michael and I'll look for Liane and Laura."

Marty rushed off as quickly as she could and June headed for the dairy kitchen, where she figured Liane and Laura would be. But instead she found only Chantal, who was sitting cross legged in the middle of her bed, reading a magazine.

"Have you seen Laura and Liane?"

"No," said Chantal without even looking up from her magazine. "They're probably outside with the horses, typical for little girls."

"But you ride, too," June blurted out. "Are you also a little girl?"

Chantal raised her head and looked at her condescendingly.

"Of course not. But just because I ride doesn't mean that I'm not interested in other things. But I guess that's not something you'd understand."

"Oh yeah?" June wished she had a good comeback. But she wasn't allowed to be rude to a camp guest and, worst of all, she couldn't think of anything to say. She was powerless in the face of Chantal's snooty manner. Without a word, she turned on her heel and went back out to the courtyard, where she saw Liane and Laura standing together outside of the Haflinger paddock. She went over to them.

Chapter 8

Liane sat up in bed and rubbed her eyes. It was only 6 a.m. and this was vacation! She threw back her blanket with a big sigh and quietly got out of bed. She could hear Laura's quiet breathing from the bunk above her. Like all the others, she was still sound asleep. Liane would be, too, if she hadn't promised June that she'd help her practice her jumps. What a relief that the alarm clock in her cell phone didn't wake the other girls.

She quickly slipped into her breeches and pulled a warm sweatshirt over her head. It was sure to be chilly this early in the morning. Liane grabbed her boots and tiptoed out the door in her socks. Outside in the courtyard, she was greeted by bright sunshine. On the distant horizon she could see the outline of snow-covered mountains. What an incredible view!

"We've got a really clear day today, eh?" she heard a voice next to her. "When the winds are dry and warm we can practically see to the state line."

Charly looked at her with a brilliant smile.

"Isn't it magnificent here?"

"You can say that again," sighed Liane. "It must be wonderful to live here. I'm jealous of June."

"Me too. But you shouldn't forget that June has a whole lot of work here. A farm like this means plenty to do," said Charly. "If she had more time for training, then she and Nelson would probably win every tournament. They are really good, you know. I could still hit myself for making her miss the last tournament."

"What happened?"

Liane recalled having heard something about this already. This time she decided she wouldn't leave Charly alone until she told her what had happened!

"You have to tell me all about it."

"If that's what you want," Charly said darkly. "To be honest, it's a little embarrassing because I acted pretty stupid then. So you have to promise me that you won't tell anyone else, okay?"

"I promise," said Liane earnestly.

"Okay, I can tell it to you on the way to the jumping course. June is already there and is probably done warming up. She'll be waiting for us."

While the two girls walked across the field behind the residence to where a few obstacles had been set up, Charly told the story of her first visit to Sunshine Farm. Liane could hardly believe that the dark-haired girl was afraid of horses at first and had found everything to be so horrible.

"And then your father became a partner here and bought Nano for you?" she asked finally. "Wow, you are so lucky."

Charly's face darkened for a moment. "Well, he had a guilty conscience because he and my mother got separated. Are your parents separated?"

Liane shook her head. What a question!

"You see, maybe I have a reason to be jealous of you."

Liane suddenly turned pensive. She had never thought of things that way. Charly had her own horse and could visit Sunshine Farm whenever she wanted to, but when she thought about it, she knew that she didn't want to switch places with her. Her own parents didn't have much time and definitely didn't have very much money, but it was a real family. And she wasn't about to trade that for anything! While she continued to think about that, Charly went over to one of the obstacles and converted a vertical into a Swedish oxer that June jumped several times from a trot. Next Charly converted it back into a vertical and raised the bar higher and higher. By this time, Maxi and Lena had also arrived so that all four of the girls were standing next to an obstacle and could

replace a bar if Nelson knocked down one of the rails, although that happened very rarely. Liane was speechless as she watched the beautiful white horse and his rider fly over the obstacles. The two of them truly were good!

"That's enough!" June called out after jumping the four obstacles two times in a row. She was out of breath. "Nelson is in fantastic form."

"When is the tournament?" asked Liane.

"Next Friday."

"Cool," Liane said joyfully. "Then I'll get to see you!"

"But only if you get up real early," said June as she took her riding helmet off her hot head. "I got the jumping schedule yesterday and it says that jumping starts at 8 a.m. That means we'll have to leave here at 5:30 a.m. at the latest. Are you sure you want to go through with that?"

Liane didn't need to think it over.

"Of course I'll come along!"

"Okay, it's a deal!" said Lena and patted her back. "Welcome to the Club of Tournament Fools."

The girls made their way to the kitchen, laughing and jabbering. Mrs. Morris had already prepared a magnificent breakfast. Liane was as hungry as a bear and gobbled up three bagels with cream cheese and tomatoes. She felt invigorated and happy as she made her way to the Haflinger paddock. She was elated yesterday when June explained to her that it was all a misunderstanding and that she could ride Navajo after all. She took the lead that hung over the gate and walked over to the chestnuts, which were standing together, grazing under the trees. Nino raised his head when he saw her coming and took a few steps in her direction. Liane suddenly had a strange feeling, almost like a guilty conscience.

"Hi there, sweetie." She lovingly stroked his soft nose. "Laura will be riding you from now on. But you'll see – she's really nice." Nino snorted and nudged her side. "Okay, okay," Liane laughed. "Here's a treat for you!" She dug a horse treat out of the pocket of her breeches and held it out to Nino on her palm. The Haflinger carefully took it with his lips and began to chew it happily. Liane ran her hand along his broad forehead and then turned to walk over to Navajo, who was still grazing under the tree. He didn't raise his head until Liane was directly next to him.

"Hi there, Navajo. I finally get to ride you now. Are you happy, too?"

Navajo turned away to eat more grass.

Liane shrugged her shoulders. What a silly question. Navajo didn't even know her yet. But she was certain that tomorrow morning he would be quite happy to see her when she got to the paddock to pick him up. At this moment, however, he seemed to be anything but pleased. It took all of Liane's strength to finally get him out to the courtyard. And it didn't get any better when she tried to ride him. When she had one foot in a stirrup and was about to pull herself up into the saddle, he simply trotted off. If Marty hadn't come and held onto him, she would've fallen in the sand.

"Thank you," she mumbled, while Marty held on to the chestnut until she could get into position in the saddle.

"Is everything okay?" Marty asked, confused. "You did want Navajo, didn't you? Or I did I mess that up again?"

"No, no," Liane shook her head. "This is fine. We just have to, um, get used to each other."

"Get used to each other?" Marty looked at Navajo skeptically. "I don't know if you can get used to Navajo. He's a little, how shall I put it, peculiar."

"That's no problem," Liane said and tried to sound as confident as she possibly could. "I know my way around Haflingers."

She pressed her heels into Navajo's sides and the powerful chestnut reluctantly set off.

"Watch where you're going!" someone yelled from behind her.

Liane turned around and recognized Chantal behind her, who had slowed Prince Pepper from a trot to a walk because Navajo was blocking the way.

"If you're walking, it's slow on the inside. Don't tell me you never learned that!"

With an arrogant expression on her face, Chantal looked at Liane from under her dark blue riding helmet and raised her eyebrows.

"Even a novice like you should know that."

Liane's face went beet red with anger and stared at her with glowering eyes. How stupid that she couldn't think of a comeback, as usual, in such situations! She just wasn't quick enough. Aside from that, though, Chantal was right. Of course she knew that anyone riding in a walk should be on the inside to make room for faster gaits. After she walked a few rounds, she took up the reins to move him into a trot. But that was easier said than done. Every time she urged Navajo into a trot, she had the feeling that he just got slower. Pretty soon, the redness in her face wasn't from anger but from exertion. But the gelding steadfastly refused to trot.

"Hold on, I'll get the crop," said Marty. "He's being especially lazy today." As Marty left the arena, Navajo walked to the middle of the arena to stand on the line in the middle. There, regardless of what Liane did, he refused to take a single step, leaving her no other choice than to wait for Marty to return. While waiting, she looked around to see what the others were doing. June was in a circle with little Lucy. Liane was impressed to see how much the girl had already improved. She sat up ramrod straight in the saddle on the Shetland pony and adapted perfectly to his rhythm.

"A natural," Liane mumbled and looked at Navajo's muscular neck. To be honest, she felt like the biggest fool. The Haflinger made her feel like an absolute beginner.

Her gaze drifted over to Laura and Nino. With a twinge of jealousy she observed that the light-colored chestnut trotted along without a problem. But she was astonished to see the grumpy expression on Laura's face. When she realized that Liane was observing her, she transitioned down to a walk and approached her.

"So how's it going with Navajo?"

Liane shrugged her shoulders.

"Okay, I guess. But he's a little lazy."

"Really?"

Laura looked at her with surprise.

"Yesterday he was a little cheeky, but not lazy. I think he's totally sweet."

"And Nino?"

"Hmm."

Laura thought for a moment.

"I don't know. I guess he's nice, but somehow… I just can't find a way to relate to him."

"Really?"

It was Liane's turn to look surprised.

"I think he's totally sweet."

"Which is how I feel about Navajo," Laura laughed.

Just then Marty returned to the arena with the crop in her hand and walked over to the girls.

Liane and Laura look at each other.

"Should we?" asked Liane.

"Without a doubt," said Laura.

When she was a few steps away from them, Marty

asked, "What is going on with you two? Why are you standing around here?"

"We wanted, er, to ask, um …" Liane began.

"… if we could trade back again," Laura completed the sentence.

Marty looked at them with widened eyes.

"Trade?"

"Yes, if I could have Navajo back and Liane could have Nino again," Laura explained.

"Does that mean I made a mistake again?" asked Marty despairingly. "Good grief, but I'm not so old as to keep confusing everything, am I?"

"No, no," Liane comforted her and gave Laura a conspiratorial look. "It's just that we changed our minds again."

Chapter 9

"Is everybody ready?"

June turned Nelson and looked around. Despite the morning's round of jumping practice, the Anglo-Arabian could barely wait for things to get started. He pranced around nervously and shook his head. June looked at all of the riders and horses that had assembled underneath the chestnut tree. Except for Maxi and little Lucy, all of them were already in the saddle. Maxi had agreed to ride on Olaf and lead Lucy on Flori. She would only be able to walk and trot, which surely wouldn't be a problem for the easygoing Norwegian who preferred to take things slowly.

Marty was on Princess, her friend Bea's beautiful

Trakehner mare. Bea had gone on vacation for a week to the Maldives so she couldn't take care of her horse.

"I think we can get going now," Marty called out to June. "You go up ahead. I'll stay in back to make sure no one gets lost."

June nodded and let out her reins. Nelson snorted with excitement and started off. June could feel his tensed muscles and looked forward to the first gallop. Liane was directly behind her with Nino. At first she couldn't believe her ears when she heard that Liane and Laura had traded back. But looking at the two of them now, it was clear that the red headed girl and the friendly Haflinger Nino were a good fit. The other riders followed in order with Chantal on Prince Pepper, Connie on Welcome, Alina on Doreen, Toni on Miss Dignified, Vicky on Ninja, Janine on Noel, Laura on Navajo, Charly on Nano, Martin on Modena, Ben on Björn the Icelandic, and Maxi on Olaf with Lucy and Flori. Marty was at the very end riding on Princess. They left the farm in a long line. Behind the riding arena, they turned off onto a narrow dirt path. June enjoyed the year's first really warm rays of sun and observed, with a sense of joy, that the trees on the edge of the path were already sprouting new leaves. The sky was a bright blue and the air had that indescribably light and pleasant scent of spring. June took a deep breath and closed her eyes. As far as she was concerned, they could ride like this all day!

"Stop! Stop!" Marty called out. "I never said anything about passing each other."

June opened her eyes and turned around. To her surprise, she saw Martin and Modena trotting past the other riders. The mare wasn't making a break for it, was she? No, that was impossible. Modena was so well trained that she would never do anything like that. Besides, if that were the case, Martin wouldn't have such a fresh smirk on his face.

"Hi." As Martin pulled up next to her, he slowed Modena down to a walk and smiled.

"What are you doing up here?" asked June, her heart pounding. "My mother can't stand it when riders pull up past each other on these trail rides."

"I was afraid of that," Martin groaned and looked back guiltily to see Marty trotting up on Princess. "But I couldn't just stay behind you the whole time without having a chance to talk to you. How are you doing?"

"Um, good I guess."

June wasn't sure which way to look. On the one hand, the situation was terribly embarrassing, but on the other, she also felt flattered that Martin wanted to be near her.

"And you?" she asked.

"Oh it's pretty nice here at Sunshine Farm. Very nice, actually. Nice people, great horses, beautiful area. But I think it's a shame that you have so little free time. There's no chance to even talk to you. I would really like to get to know you better, you know?"

June wasn't sure how to deal with someone so

disarmingly open. But she didn't have to think it over for long, because Marty had caught up with them and was slowing Princess to a walk.

"Would you mind telling me what you were thinking?" she asked angrily. "You can't just pass other riders as you please. Think about what could happen if the horses made a break for it and someone were to fall off."

Martin suddenly looked very remorseful.

"Oh gosh, I hadn't thought about that. Honest, I didn't want anything like that to happen. I just wanted to be able to talk to June."

"To talk to June?"

Marty looked mistrustfully at Martin then at June then back to Martin.

"Alright then," she said finally. "If you want to talk to June, then do it after our trail ride, okay? And now see to it that you get back to where you were."

"Okay," said Martin and turned Modena back. Then he turned his head to June. "Ciao bella, it was nice to talk to you."

June blushed bright red and looked at him with her jaw hanging down.

"Ciao bella," Liane giggled behind her. "Oh my gosh, he's totally into you."

"Don't be silly," June growled and took up Nelson's reins. "Look over there – that's the place where we'll start trotting. We're going to get ready to trot, pass it on to the others."

Without waiting for an answer, June started into a trot. Was Liane right? Did he really like her? June shook her head. This guy had her totally confused! Before the path narrowed and led into a small patch of forest, she took up the reins and turned around to Liane. "Tell the person behind you that we'll be transitioning to a walk now. She reined back Nelson and steered him through the trees. She had to keep bending forward onto her white horse's neck to avoid being hit by a low branch. It was so quiet in the woods that the only thing you could hear was the crackling of the dry twigs that the horses stepped on. After a while, June could see a small opening ahead that led them out of the woods. When she got there, she stopped and waited until the others had caught up. Considering how narrow the path was and all the low branches, it would have been pretty unpleasant if one of the horses decided to start trotting through the woods just to catch up with the others.

They didn't start riding again until Marty gave the command. Before long they would reach the field where the Haflingers frolicked yesterday after they broke out. June looked around tensely. Hopefully they wouldn't run into Farmer Myers. He didn't have a right to forbid them to ride on this path. Still, she didn't feel like running into the permanently cranky farmer. But she did want to use the opportunity to see for herself what the field looked like now. Marty swore that it had been completely destroyed. She was pretty worried that Farmer Myers would sue her, and unfortunately Charly's father was in New York for two weeks on an important business trip. Of all times!

As they got closer to the field where she had desperately tried to round up the Haflinger Gang yesterday, June couldn't believe her eyes. The grain really had been trampled flat in so many places. How strange that she hadn't noticed that yesterday! No wonder Farmer Myers was so furious and wanted to sue them.

June rode on, deep in thought and kept trying to figure out how the Haflingers could cause so much damage in so little time. Although she had grown very fond of the powerful chestnuts with the blonde manes, she did ask herself every so often if Sunshine Farm wouldn't be better off without them. It was almost unbearable how much trouble five – well, four now – horses were capable of making.

Brrrrummmmm!

A loud noise suddenly interrupted her thoughts. Startled, she raised her head and saw horses run past her on both sides. Although Nelson would have loved to join them, she held the reins so tightly that he pranced nervously in place. It took her a few seconds to realize that Prince Pepper, Welcome, Navajo and Ninja had been spooked by the loud noise and bolted. Uncertain of what she should do, June looked toward her mother.

"Follow them to the field, but not too close!" called Marty. "Nelson is so fast he'll catch up to them. Then you can move up to the front and try to make them stop."

June nodded and galloped off. This was the kind of job Nelson liked best. In broad, rhythmic strides, he raced across the field and bit-by-bit caught up with the horses that bolted and then blocked their way. Prince Pepper, who galloped at the front of the group, was so surprised that Chantal seized the opportunity to slow him down. In turn, Connie, Janine and Vicky were also able to slow their horses and get them back under control.

"Wow!" Connie beamed, her head bright red as she rode back to the rest of the group. "That was cool. I've never galloped that fast before."

"I'd just like to know what idiot made all that noise," Chantal complained. "We should read him the riot act."

"That's for sure," June agreed with her – just his once. "If you want, you can do it yourself. Because there they are."

They heard the noise again and then saw two motorcycles race across the field.

"This is ridiculous!" Chantal screamed as Prince Pepper began to prance again.

"Just relax the reins a little and stay next to Nelson," said June. "He'll calm down soon enough."

In fact, the chestnut calmed down so much that he simply stayed at Nelson's side. He snorted somewhat excitedly and tossed his head, but at least he didn't try to bolt again.

"Are you guys out of your minds?" June asked when she reached the group of motorcycle riders. It was four teenagers, three boys and a girl.

"What do you mean?" asked one of them and then revved his engine extra loud so that Prince Pepper took a few steps to the side. "Don't tell me your horsies are afraid of us."

"Can't you just turn those bikes off?" June shouted. She didn't like this situation. "What are you doing here, anyway?"

"What're we doing here?" The rider with the silver helmet looked up at her. "We heard that a good friend of ours was here on vacation and we wanted to stop by to say hello."

"A good friend?"

June frowned.

"And who is that supposed to be?"

The rider looked up at the group on horseback that stood a few feet away from him.

"There she is. Hi there, Liane!"

He let the motor rev up and rode a little closer to the group.

"Pretty surprised, eh?"

"What are you doing here?" Liane asked, astonished, and looked at him with an expression of shock.

Chapter 10

If a giant green monster with four eyes and eight legs had crawled out of the field at that moment, Liane wouldn't have been more frightened. At first she couldn't believe her eyes. But once she heard Robin's voice, she knew that her imagination wasn't playing tricks on her. Unfortunately. Suddenly she felt like she was in the middle of a horrible nightmare. And she had so looked forward to this vacation.

"What am I doing here?" Robin laughed bitterly. "I'm spending my vacation with my cousins because I wasn't allowed to go to Italy with my soccer team. To be honest, I'm extremely mad at you for that. You didn't really think I'd let you off the hook so easily, did you?"

"And how did you know that I was here?"

Liane was so confused that she couldn't think straight.

"Because I read in your stupid horse magazine that the riding camp was close to where my cousins live. I was hoping that I'd meet up with you here. Because since you ruined my vacation, why shouldn't I ruin yours? So consider yourself warned, matchstick. I'm sure we'll meet each other again over the next few days."

He revved the motor again and quickly rode back to the other motorcycle before the two vehicles raced back along the dirt path. Liane stared after them until they were no longer visible.

"Liane? Are you okay? You look like you just saw a ghost."

As if in a trance, Liane turned to Connie, who was standing directly behind her with Welcome.

"Er, no, although, in a way, yes."

Connie looked so confused that Liane had to smile despite her fright.

"Unfortunately I know those guys – or rather, I know two of them. They go to my school."

"And what do they want from you?"

In the meantime, June had caught up to the rest of the group and looked inquisitively at Liane.

"To be honest, it didn't exactly sound like they were buddies of yours."

Liane swallowed hard.

"No they definitely aren't friends of mine. Robin picks on me all the time. His twin sister isn't so bad, but she does whatever he tells her."

Liane sounded so pathetic that June smiled at her sympathetically.

"You poor thing. That really sounds awful. But I think that my mother would like us to continue riding. We'll talk it all over when we're back at the farm."

Liane nodded and quickly got in place behind June. Marty trotted up to them with Princess.

"Do you have any idea what kind of people they are, June?"

Liane held her breath and observed June. Would she blab to her mother that the whole problem was because of her? June understood and shook her head.

"I have no idea, but we'll figure it out soon enough, won't we, Liane?" She smiled conspiratorially at Liane, who gave her a look of gratitude in return.

"Okay then, let's continue. What a relief that no one fell. Imagine what would have happened if Olaf had bolted, too. I don't think Lucy could have held on to Flori if that had happened."

Marty let her gaze wander and observed the torn-up field.

"Oh my, would you just take a look at what the Haflingers did this time? If I only knew what we could do to calm down Farmer Myers."

"I could have sworn," said June, "that it didn't look so bad yesterday."

"You probably didn't look very closely because you had to catch all the Haflingers. The only thing I know is that this time we are in serious trouble," Marty groaned, turned her Trakehner mare and trotted back to the end of the group. The rest of their trail ride was uneventful and Liane was relieved when they reached the farm and she could hide a little in the farthest corner of the stables as she unsaddled Nino. Oh no, this was so embarrassing!

"Oh, Nino." Liane rubbed her face into the Haflinger's blonde mane and breathed in his sweet smell. The gelding stood still as a statue as if to prop her up. That made Liane feel better and she lovingly stroked the golden hair on his neck. "You really are a nice horse. Please don't be angry with me for not recognizing that right away." Nino snorted and pressed his big, soft nose into her middle. Liane laughed and pulled a treat out of her pocket and watched with satisfaction as the Haflinger chewed with pleasure. But then a shadow crossed her face. For a minute she had completely forgotten what had happened earlier. She had to talk to June and explain to her again that she had nothing to do with those people. She quickly cleaned Nino's coat and then brought him up to the paddock where his four Haflinger colleagues were already waiting for him. Then she found June on the bench under the big chestnut tree, where she was sitting with Charly, Martin and Ben, all relaxing and drinking bottles of soda.

"Would you like one?" Ben asked and, without waiting for an answer, put it on the table.

"Thanks," said Liane and sat down on the bench next to Charly.

"Well?" June looked at her inquisitively. "Who were those guys?"

Liane shrugged her shoulders.

"I only know two of them. Robin, the guy who did the talking, and Marita, the girl who was sitting on the back of his motorcycle. Both of them go to my school."

"And the other two?"

"I don't know them. At least I don't think I do. When they wear their helmets you can barely tell them apart. Maybe they're the cousins that Robin was talking about."

"And what did that guy mean when he said he was going to ruin your vacation because you ruined his?"

Slowly and with many pauses, Liane began to tell about moving, about her new school and mostly about her trouble with Marita and Robin. The longer she talked, the more the words seemed to just fly out of her mouth. Suddenly it didn't matter to her what the others would think of her. The only thing that was important was that she could finally talk. Ever since she moved to Washington, DC, she hadn't had an opportunity to get all that off her chest. June, Charly, Martin and Ben listened attentively until she finished her story.

"You poor thing!" said Charly, laying her arm around her shoulder sympathetically. "That all sounds just awful. And what lousy luck that their cousins live nearby."

"It's enough to make me lose my mind," Liane mumbled. "And I was so looking forward to this vacation because I wouldn't have to see them for a while. And now they've followed me here and are going to ruin my trip."

"Oh that's just silly," said June decisively, slamming her soda bottle onto the table. "We won't let them ruin your vacation. If they show up here one more time, then we'll show them something!"

"That's really nice of you," said Liane, "but what do you want to do to them? They're older than we are and the two other guys didn't exactly look small and weak."

"Liane is right," said Ben. "I don't think we can fight them. I'd say we don't have much of a chance against them."

"And what if we call the police?" Charly asked hopefully.

June shook her head.

"Nah, they don't come unless something has already happened. You can't ban them from driving around the area."

For a moment, there was total silence. Then Martin slammed his hand on the table and jumped up from the bench.

"Maybe you can't ban them from driving around the area, but you can definitely forbid them from driving through the fields. Did you see what they did? They destroyed everything. Can you imagine how angry the farmer will be when he finds out who did that?!"

"Oh that." June dismissed him with her hand. "Unfortunately he already knows. It was our Haflingers, who ran through his field again yesterday. Those beasts use every chance they get to break through the fence and churn up Farmer Myers' fields. I think we really have a problem this time. He told my mother that he plans to sue us." She turned to Charly. "It's high time for your dad to get back so I can have a talk with him. Myers doesn't take my mother very seriously." She blew a strand of hair out of her face and looked disgusted. "Typical man."

"Hey, hey, hey!" exclaimed Martin. "But that's not true for all men – is it?"

"Wait a second, June," Liane said, ignoring Martin's joke. "Didn't you say that the field didn't look half that bad when you rounded up the Haflingers?"

June nodded.

"I didn't think it did. And I couldn't figure out why Farmer Myers was making such a big deal of it this time."

"Does that mean that the field wasn't in such bad shape yesterday when you left?" asked Martin.

"It didn't seem that way to me."

"Oh my gosh, now I understand what you're getting

at!" exclaimed Ben excitedly. "Just think back for a minute, June. You didn't think the field was such a mess, but then later, Farmer Myers called up to tell you that everything had been destroyed."

"Yes? What are you saying?"

"In other words, it must have happened after you left with the Haflingers."

"What do you mean?"

"Well, someone must have come after you left and churned up the field."

"Are you trying to say that Liane's, er, acquaintances did it?" June asked slowly.

The others nodded.

"But shouldn't there be tire tracks, then?"

"Maybe nobody looked for them because the farmer was so sure that it was the Haflingers," said Martin thoughtfully.

"Besides, since we haven't had any rain, the ground is rock hard, so that there aren't really any tracks to see," added Ben.

"But why would they have done something like that?" June still couldn't believe that someone would purposely drive through a field on a motorcycle.

"Maybe because they think it's fun?" Martin suggested. "I have no idea what people like that think, but that might be the reason."

"That's all fine and good," said Liane, "But even if that is what really happened, how are we going to prove that it wasn't the Haflingers?"

"By catching the other guys red-handed," said Martin. He looked at the group with an adventurous sparkle in his eye. "Judging by what Liane just told us, they're sure to turn up here again, if only to ruin her vacation."

"Then we're only missing one thing," said Charly. Everyone looked at her.

"A plan."

Chapter 11

June gingerly opened the door and peeked out through a narrow crack. The courtyard was quiet and empty.

"Do you see anyone?" Charly asked from behind her.

"No, there doesn't seem to be anyone around."

Carefully the girls slipped into their riding boots and sneaked across the courtyard, past the smaller building in the direction of the sand ring. Ben and Martin were waiting for them at the entrance. June looked around.

"Where's Liane?"

"No idea," said Martin. "Maybe she fell asleep. If she doesn't come soon, though, we should just leave without her."

"No," June said assertively. "I can't believe she would have fallen asleep. This is too important to her to let us go without her. Let's wait a little longer. I'm sure she'll be here soon."

June was right. After they waited another five minutes or so, a small figure approached them in the dark.

"Hi," said Liane. "I'm sorry it took me so long, but Janine and Vicky just didn't want to fall asleep. They were talking the whole time about how sweet Noel and Ninja are." She turned to the two boys. "How did you two get out, anyway? Didn't you have to go through our room?"

"Piece of cake," Ben smiled. "We went out the window, of course."

Charly began to stamp her foot impatiently.

"Isn't it time for us to get moving? It's pretty darn creepy out here in the dark and I would much rather be in my bed right now."

"Ahem." June cleared her throat. "Then let's get going. It's quite a distance on foot."

"It's too bad we can't take the horses," said Ben regretfully. "Old Björn would probably enjoy a trail ride in the dark."

"No thanks." June shuddered as she thought back to the last night ride, when she had such a bad fall from her horse that she broke her shoulder.

"Besides, we'd attract too much attention. Maybe the horses would neigh or someone would hear the sound of hooves and then everyone would know what we were up to."

"But what's so bad about that?" Charly asked. "We're not doing anything illegal."

"No, but can you imagine how upset my mother would be if she found out that we went to Farmer Myers' field to look for clues? It's much better if she doesn't find out about it. And if the others know, then we run the risk of somebody blabbing. She's really nervous these days."

"Hasn't she reached your father yet?" Ben asked Charly. "I'm sure he'll be able to work it all out once he talks to the farmer."

"When he has the time," said Charly with an undertone of sarcasm. "When my father's around, he takes care of everything. The problem is, he's usually not around …"

She paused and an embarrassed silence settled on the group.

"June is right," said Ben quickly. "Until we have incontrovertible evidence, we shouldn't tell anyone. Okay then, what are we waiting for? Let's get going!"

The moon was high in the sky and bathed the landscape in an unreal silver light. June took a deep breath and looked over to the treetops at the edge of the woods that gently swayed in the wind. It really was beautiful here at Sunshine Farm! Especially since they didn't have any financial worries anymore since Charly's father became a partner. It would all be so nice if only they weren't constantly having altercations with Farmer Myers. She marched on resolutely and showed the others a shortcut through the woods they could only take on foot because after the woods they'd come to a meadow with a fence. Once they reached the fence, Charly turned around nervously.

"Are you sure there's nothing in the meadow?"

"What are you talking about?" June asked. She hadn't even thought about that.

"I don't know. Cows, maybe… or bulls!"

June laughed, although the question made her nervous.

"Don't be silly. I know Farmer Myers has a few cows, but no bulls. And even if he does, I'm sure he puts them in the barn at night."

"I hope you're right," sighed Charly as she climbed through the fence. The others followed her.

"What's that light back there?" asked Martin after they had gone a few yards.

"That's Farmer Myers' house," June answered. "But don't worry, he can't see us out here in the dark. And we won't switch on our flashlights until we're out in the field." She reached into the pocket of her jeans to reassure herself that the flashlight she took out of the kitchen drawer was still in there.

"Are you totally sure?" asked Charly, who had already experienced several of Farmer Myers' fits of anger first hand. "I'm already afraid of him in the daytime. If I were to meet him in the dark I'm sure I'd just faint."

"Why don't you relax a little," said June, amused.

"You don't think he grows fangs in the dark, do you? Like a werewolf?" She laughed.

Grrrrrrr!

"What was that?" Liane squealed and grabbed on to June's arm. "Did you hear that? It sounded like something growling!"

June wasn't laughing anymore. The noise really did sound like a growl.

Grrrrrr!

"Up ahead," whispered Ben and pointed to a black something that was slowly approaching them in the dark. June was scared silly. She would've liked nothing better than to turn on her heel and run back to the woods as quickly as possible.

"Oh no," mumbled Martin and backed up a few steps. "It really does look like a werewolf. Or like a Hound of the Baskervilles. Whatever, it looks dangerous."

In front of them stood a huge, longhaired sheepdog. Its eyes glowed eerily in the moonlight. It moved closer and growled again.

"That's Farmer Myers' dog," whispered June uneasily. "I didn't think he let him walk around out here at night. What do we do now?"

The dog stopped and stared at them. June had the feeling that he would attack them any second now unless they did something fast…

"Killer! Come here right now! Bad dog, you're always trying to hunt!"

The dog turned his head in the direction of the voice and then looked back at June and her friends who were observing him tensely. Would he obey his owner? The dog hesitated, then turned around. He looked back at them one more time and then reluctantly trotted back to the house.

"Whew!" moaned Charley with relief once the animal had disappeared. "I was so scared I almost wet my pants."

"You can say that again." June was surprised to hear a shiver in her voice. "Did you hear what the dog's name is? Killer! He probably wouldn't have been very gentle with us. We would've been something like a light midnight snack for him. Now let's get out of here!"

They ran as fast as they could, clear across the meadow to the field that the Haflingers supposedly destroyed. They climbed through the fence and then checked to be sure that the farmer's house really wasn't visible from where they were, then turned on their flashlights and started to search. It wasn't long before Ben discovered the first tracks.

"Take a look at this!"

The others walked over too, anxious with excitement.

"Those are clearly tire tracks. And not from a tractor – they're much too narrow for that. These tracks were made by a motorcycle."

"That's excellent," Liane was happy. "Tomorrow we can point these out to Farmer Myers and explain to him who was responsible for all the damage. Then he'll know that the Haflingers weren't at fault."

Unfortunately it isn't that easy," said June. "The tracks prove that motorcycles were on the field, but Farmer Myers will still maintain that the Haflingers did the damage first."

"You're right," said Ben. "Besides, he could claim that we were the ones who made the tracks after the fact in order to deflect attention from the Haflingers. It would be typical for the nasty old geezer to accuse us of that."

"Does that mean that we snuck out of the house in the middle of the night – for nothing?" asked Liane, with disappointment in her voice. "Why didn't we just stay in our beds, then?"

"Of course it wasn't for nothing," said June. "Now we know for sure that those guys were in the field with their motorcycles. And not just up front where they ambushed us on our trail ride, but all the way back here, too. Now we just have to find a way to prove it."

"But that's simple," said Martin. "We just have to catch them red-handed, hold on to them and then get the farmer."

"Real simple," said Charly and grinned sarcastically. "Are we supposed to stake them out day and night? Just to give Killer the opportunity to really catch us?"

"Well, we would need a little luck," said Martin, taking offense. "But I don't know what else we can do. Do you?"

June, Charly and Liane looked at each helplessly and shook their heads.

"Oh come on," groaned Ben. "The answer is as plain as day."

"Quit with your strange jokes and just tell us what you're thinking," June said with annoyance. In her opinion, the situation was much too serious to makes jokes about!

"Now think for a minute about why those guys are even here… because they want to torment Liane. That means that we don't have to look for them because they'll pop up again pretty soon anyway. That Robin guy said himself that they'd be back. And these paths here near the farm look like the best ones for motorcycles anyway – much better that any of the paths through the woods or meadows. Which means that we'll meet up with them again here – and when we do, we'll be ready for them and hold on to them until the farmer comes."

June looked at Ben with admiration. She never would have thought of that herself, but saw that he was totally right.

"In other words, we'll ride this way every day and wait for them?"

Ben nodded.

"And I have a feeling that we won't have to wait very long before those guys show up again."

Chapter 11

"Don't you plan to wake up at all this morning, June?"

Marty stood impatiently next to June's bed and touched her shoulder.

"Is there something wrong with you? Do you feel sick?"

She looked at June nervously.

"That's the last thing I need, for you to get sick this week."

June sat up slowly and rubbed her eyes.

"No, I'm just tired," she comforted her mother. "I, um, just couldn't fall asleep last night."

"That's a relief." Marty sounded like the weight of the

world had just been lifted off her shoulders. June could sympathize with her. When they had camp guests, there was so much to do at Sunshine Farm that despite having a financial partner and help from Mrs. Morris, it was nothing less than a catastrophe if anyone couldn't do her job. Of course, she couldn't exactly tell her mother that the reason why she couldn't fall asleep was because she was too busy looking for motorcycle tracks in Farmer Myers' field.

Exactly! The tire tracks in Farmer Myers' field! She had to make sure that their trail ride this afternoon would lead past there again. That shouldn't be all too hard, because although it could be unpleasant if they met up with the cranky old farmer, that was where the best riding trails were. So she wouldn't have to worry about Marty getting suspicious if they rode in that direction another time. Maybe they'd get lucky and those guys would show up there again in the afternoon. But June didn't know how they could be sure that Farmer Myers would be there at the right time too, but she knew they'd think of something in time.

When June walked into the kitchen, she saw that the others were already seated at the table, grabbing hungrily at the fresh rolls Mrs. Morris had bought at the bakery on the way over to Sunshine Farm. June sat down on the only free chair, between Charly and Chantal, and took a big sip of orange juice from the glass next to her plate. Most of the conversations at the table were about horses and about what they planned to do that day.

"After breakfast, you can get the horses from the paddock and give them a thorough grooming," said Marty. "Then the two groups will have their riding lessons separately, one after the other so that the arena isn't as full as it was yesterday. First the advanced group and then the others." She smiled a little sheepishly. "I still have to get used to having so many guests here."

"And in the afternoon?" asked Chantal, as she tossed her long black hair over her shoulder. With a brief twinge of envy, June noticed that she really did have beautiful hair. Martin, who was sitting across from her and watching her the whole time, looked like he was thinking the same thing. June got a strange feeling again in her stomach that made her uncomfortable. Could it be possible that Martin like conceited Chantal? She bit her lower lip. Good grief, June, she thought to herself. What is going on with you? You aren't jealous, are you? It was all she could do to stop looking at Chantal and concentrate on what her mother was saying.

"And this afternoon we'll go on another trail ride."

"Another trail ride?" groaned Chantal. "Not again! Can't we do something else? It's so boring to keep doing the same things over and over again."

"Why did you even come here if you think riding is boring?" asked June sharply, giving her a dirty look.

"June, please."

Marty looked at her sternly.

"I don't think riding is boring," said Chantal coldly.
"I just think it's boring to keep doing the same things. If
we have riding lessons again this morning, then we could
do something this afternoon that has nothing to do with
riding."

"And what do you have in mind?" asked Marty
politely.

Chantal was obviously waiting to be asked that
question.

"Well, we could all go to Splash, which is supposed to
be near here."

June groaned to herself. Why did Chantal have to
bring up this idea today? She had nothing against the idea
of going to the big water park – but not today, the day
that they wanted to prove that it wasn't the Haflingers
that had destroyed the field.

"All right! Let's go to Splash!" exclaimed Janine. "I
heard of that place. It's supposed to be totally excellent!"

"Doesn't it have a giant slide?" asked Connie.

"Yeah, it has two even. And whirlpools, a warm
water pool – oh, it just has everything," Chantal said
enthusiastically and looked at June triumphantly. "On the
registration form it said that we should bring along our
bathing suits and towels."

June looked across the table at Liane who appeared
to be at least as disgusted as she was. She opened
her mouth, but before she could say anything, Marty
announced, "Okay then, why not? The horses will have

the afternoon off and we'll go to Splash. But now off to your horses, because I want you to really earn it before I take you to cool off in the pool."

They all got up from the table happily and raced out to the courtyard to get their horses from the paddock. June and Liane follow them slowly.

"What a bummer," said Liane when they reached the stairs and were out of earshot of the others.

"What day is today, anyway?"

"Sunday," answered June. "Why do you ask?"

"Monday, Tuesday, Wednesday, Thursday," Liane counted the days on her fingers. "That's not much time when you think about how quickly a week passes."

June nodded.

"You're right. And then suddenly it's Friday and you have to leave without having had a chance to prove that it wasn't the Haflingers that tore up that field. It really is a huge problem for us. But it would be good for you if you didn't have to see those guys again this week."

"No way." Liane shook her head wildly. "Not at all. Because I think it's totally mean that the Haflingers are being blamed for something they didn't even do."

She was quiet for a moment before she continued. "Say June, you aren't really going to get rid of the Haflingers, are you?"

"I have no idea," said June uncertainly. "If we have serious trouble because of them and Charly's father decides that they're causing us financial problems …"

109

she sighed and shrugged her shoulders. "I really don't know."

"Don't you see? That's why we have to catch those jerks red-handed. I definitely don't want the Haflingers to get sold. Who knows where they'll end up and what'll happen to them there." Liane shuddered at the thought. "We can't lose a single day, do you understand, June? Is there some way that we can stay here today?"

At the bottom of the stairs they pulled on their riding boots and walked across the courtyard. June thought for a while. What Liane had just said was true. If they wanted to catch the guys red handed, then they couldn't afford to waste any time.

"Hmm, maybe we can tell my mother that since I want to practice for the tournament, there's no way I can come swimming. You can say that you'd rather stay here and help me train."

June let out a long sigh.

"And that's not even a lie. I desperately need to train so that I don't make a fool of myself on Friday in front of all those people."

"Great!" exclaimed Liane. "Then we really can do some training and afterward we'll go on the trail. What do you think of that?"

June looked at her gratefully.

"Would you really do that? That would be truly great."

"Of course," said Liane and gave her a friendly pat on the back. "After all, I'd like to watch you win."

"Okay, then I'll go ask my mother and you can go get Nino from the paddock so you aren't late for riding lessons."

June found her mother at the riding arena where she was raking away the hoof marks.

She wasn't exactly thrilled with the idea of both girls staying, but in the end she decided to allow it.

"At least that makes two seats fewer for me to worry about," she groaned and leaned on the top of the rake with both hands. "I've had to ask Mrs. Morris to drive over twice because there isn't room for everyone in our two cars. But that means that we won't have a warm dinner tonight because she won't have enough time to cook something. And all of that because of Chantal." Marty rolled her eyes. "I had no idea that running a riding camp would be this complicated."

June couldn't suppress a grin. That was typical of her mother. First full speed ahead on an adventure, only to realize later what she had gotten herself into.

"And the situation with the Haflingers is surely going to drive me nuts," Marty continued. She looked over at the paddock where Liane was just walking by with Nino. "If they don't stop the foolishness soon, I'm going to have to take action."

"Don't worry about it," June said quickly and hugged her mother. "We'll find a solution. You just worry about giving your lesson now." The last thing she wanted was for her mother to start talking about how the Haflingers had to go.

She and Liane just had to catch those guys to give the Haflingers a clean slate! With determination in her stride, she walked back to the courtyard to the hitching post where Lucy and Florid were waiting for her. As soon as she saw the little girl's joyful smile, all her cares disappeared as if by magic. Lucy truly was a gem and it was lovely to see how happy she was when she rode around on old Flori. Marty was right; running a riding camp was pretty darned complicated, but it also was a lot of fun. At least as long as the guests were as enthusiastic and good-natured as Lucy.

"Come on now and just hold still for once!"

June turned around to Chantal, who was trying to shove the bit into Prince Pepper's mouth. Generally the gelding was very cooperative, but today he didn't seem to be in the mood to have the metal piece in his mouth, so he held his head as high as he could. June sympathized with him. She'd defend herself, too, if someone kept pulling on her mouth every day. After this week, Marty would have her hands full convincing the lovely chestnut to be a little more relaxed with riders again.

Chapter 12

"Are they finally gone?"

Ben slipped out through the partially opened front door and went over to the others. Liane, June, Charly and Martin all nodded.

"Whew, that sure took long enough. So, are we ready to go?"

"Training comes first," said Liane.

"Training?" asked Martin.

"Of course. June has to train for the tournament."

"I thought that was just an excuse," said Martin. "So that we wouldn't have to go along."

"It was," said Liane. "But if June is going to

participate in the tournament on Friday, then she needs to be ready for it. We'll help her first and then we'd all ride off together."

"But we have to be back here on time," said June. "My mother will blow her top if she finds out that we went out riding without an adult."

"Then hurry up and get your horse ready so we can head out as soon as possible," said Ben. "In the meantime, the rest of us can start grooming so when you're done with training all we have to do is saddle up."

Liane went with Charly to the Haflinger paddock where Nino and Nano stood grazing with the others.

"I think it's really great that you guys stayed here," said Liane.

"Now wait a minute." Charly looked at her from the side and shook her head. "There's no way that we'd leave you alone with this business. Besides, I'd much rather be here with Nano. When I'm in DC, I can go swimming any time I want."

"You live in Washington, DC, too?" Liane looked at Charly with surprise. "Where exactly?"

"In Georgetown," said Charly.

Liane nodded. She should have guessed that Charly, whose father obviously had a lot of money, would live in one of the best neighborhoods in the city.

"And you?" asked Charly. "Where do you live?"

"In Woodley Park," answered Liane a little bashfully. Her parents didn't earn as much money, which is why they lived in a neighborhood that was much less upscale.

"But that's cool!" exclaimed Charly. "Woodley Park isn't at all far from Georgetown. We could meet up after school sometime and go see a movie together or something. What do you think?"

"Would you really like to do that?" asked Liane happily.

"Of course. I'd be so happy to have someone in the city that I can talk to about horses," Charly smiled. "And not just any horses – Haflingers! We'll have to trade phone numbers later."

Charly walked over to Nano and lovingly stroked his shiny neck.

Liane continued on to Nino and hooked the lead onto his bridle. She could hardly believe her luck! She finally wouldn't feel quite so alone in Washington now that she knew she could meet up with someone after school who had exactly the same interests as she did. She owed all that to Sunshine Farm, which was why she had to help to make sure that the Haflingers would be allowed to stay!

After all of the horses were thoroughly groomed, they continued on to the jumping field where June was already galloping around the circle.

"Are you ready?" Ben called out to her and went over to the vertical that he was transforming into a Swedish oxer. June nodded and adjusted her helmet.

She trotted with Nelson to the obstacle and he casually jumped over it.

"I think you can make that a little higher next time," said June. "Nelson is in good spirits."

Liane observed and admired how June steered the hot-tempered Anglo-Arabian through the small show jumping course. Even Martin, who stood next to her, couldn't take his eyes off of June. Liane had to be careful not to laugh out loud. She could swear that the boy with the dark blonde curls and the friendly smile had a crush on June. And if she weren't completely off base, it looked like June had a crush on him, too. At any rate, she always seemed to be pretty happy when she was around him.

After June had taken all the obstacles twice, she slowed the white horse down to a walk and left the reins long.

"If he's in this kind of form on Friday, then nothing can go wrong."

She hugged Nelson's neck joyfully.

"You really are the best horse in the world!"

A short time later, the others had also saddled up their horses and headed off for Farmer Myers' fields. After they had ridden for a while, they saw another rider on a big brown horse off in the distance.

"Who is that?" asked Liane.

June squinted.

"That must be Mr. Kessler. He boards his horse at our stable," she explained. "I only hope that we don't meet up with him or he'll wind up telling my mother that we were out riding alone."

"What's so bad about that anyway?" asked Martin. "Aren't we old enough?"

"It wouldn't normally be a problem," said June. "Ben and I often go for rides alone. But you're camp guests and my mother wants everything to be well-ordered during riding camp so that we don't get a bad reputation, along the lines of 'they let their camp guests out to ride without adequate supervision by trained personnel.' That could be a real problem for us."

"What do you mean, 'no trained personnel'?" Martin didn't want to understand the problem. "You're a good rider – that's something you just proved to us in training."

"Er, thanks," June blushed and wasn't sure how to respond to a compliment like that.

"But June isn't a trained instructor," Ben came to her aid. "Besides, she isn't an adult, either. If something bad were to happen, we'd have a real problem on our hands."

"And my mother has enough worries because of the Haflingers," said June and made a face. "That's why we have to be sure that no one finds out we were out here alone."

Before long they reached Farmer Myers' fields and looked around. There was no sign of any motorcycles. Ben looked at his watch.

"It's 3:30. On our afternoon rides we usually pass

by here around this time. So I wonder what's keeping them."

"Why are you so sure that they know exactly when we go on our trail rides?" asked Liane.

"We aren't sure," said Ben, "but they must have found out somehow that Sunshine Farm organizes trail rides that lead past this field. And since we usually go out for a ride at about the same time every day during camp, it's pretty easy for them to figure out what time we come past here."

"From the farmers in the area, for instance," said June. "Or from the people in the village. After all, we live in the country and everybody knows what everyone else is up to."

"Well then," Charly piped in. "What will we do now? Do we want to wait?"

"I don't think we have any other choice," muttered June. Although she couldn't have described what it was she was expecting, she nevertheless was disappointed that there was no one around.

"Do you really think that's a good idea?" asked Martin. "If we wait here, they're sure to know that we've planned something against them. They have to believe that they can surprise us."

"Martin is right," said Ben. "But what should we do then?"

"Keep riding," suggested Martin. "Really slowly. Maybe they're nearby already and just waiting for us.

Try not to keep looking around for them and just act like we're having a normal conversation."

June rode next to Martin and tried to act as if she was having an exciting conversation. In reality, she kept asking herself if they were being observed from somewhere. She had to force herself to not turn around. Martin told her about his life in Baltimore – his school and his soccer team, and how he was gone almost every weekend traveling to games.

"That doesn't leave much time for riding," he said and winked at June, "which is a shame when you think about all the nice people you can meet that way."

He guided Modena to walk very close to Nelson so that his knee was touching June's. June felt her heart jump into her throat.

"Maybe I should come to Sunshine Farm more often for vacation… what do you think?"

"Oh, er, um yes, why not?" June croaked and simultaneously felt incredibly stupid. Why did she always have to act so dumb whenever Martin was near her? He had to think that she was incapable of saying a correct sentence! On the other hand, she really liked the idea of seeing Martin at Sunshine Farm more often.

"We, er, could maybe …"

She didn't get any farther because they suddenly heard a loud noise and two motorcycles burst out from behind the bushes at the edge of the path. Modena bolted and Nelson took a huge jump to the side. Before June knew

what was happening, she was thrown from the saddle and landed on the dusty path with a loud thud. I have to hold the reins tightly, she thought, and felt a burning sensation in her hands as the reins slipped through her fingers. And then suddenly everything went black.

Chapter 13

"June? Are you okay, June?"

June opened her eyes and looked into the worried faces of Martin and Ben.

"What happened?" she whispered and groaned. She would probably be covered with bruises from falling on the hard ground. Slowly she moved her arms and then her legs. Please, please let nothing be broken, she prayed. Please not again. I so want to participate in the tournament this time. But it felt as if nothing was broken.

"How many fingers do you see?"

June looked at the two fingers Ben held directly in front of her nose.

"Two, of course. What's that for?"

"I just wanted to see if you had a concussion or something," said Ben, taking offense.

June slowly sat up.

"What happened anyway? And where is Nelson?"

Ben and Martin look at each other.

"Those idiots were here again," Martin said finally. "The horses were startled and you fell."

"I can feel that," June groaned. Every movement hurt. She stood up on wobbly legs.

"Where are the other two? And where is Nelson?"

"Nelson ran off," said Ben and, when he saw the shocked expression on her face, added quickly, "Charly and Liane went off after him. They'll be back with him any minute now."

"Ran off?" June screamed. She completely forgot about her pain and only wanted to know where her horse was. "Where are those stupid jerks? If I get my hands on them..."

"They zoomed off again," said Ben. "I wanted to chase after them, but they were so fast that I didn't have the slightest chance with Björn."

"And I jumped right off my horse to see how you were," said Martin. "I was so worried when I saw you lying on the ground like that."

"I'm okay," said June quietly as she clapped the dust off of her breeches. Where in the world could Nelson be? What if he hurt himself? What if he ran to the road?

Suddenly she was overwhelmed with thoughts of all the terrible things that could happen to a horse running through the area without a rider.

"And those horrible guys just drove off?" June balled her hands into fists. "We have to do something. Right away!"

"Now calm down first," said Ben. "Let's wait for Charly and Liane to come back."

"No," said June. "That'll take too long. Besides, they don't know their way around here as well as I do."

She walked over to Modena and put her foot into the stirrup.

"You two can wait for them here and I'll go look for Nelson."

With that she swung herself into the saddle and galloped off. What direction could Nelson have gone? She decided to ride toward the big road that was only a few miles away. If he had run off that way, then maybe she could head him off first. Modena galloped across the field in fast, even strides toward the woods. She'd have to cut the tempo then to keep from slamming her head into low-hanging branches. As the path got narrower and narrower, she slowed the mare to a trot. There! There was something up ahead! June could see something light-colored flash between the trees. She trotted over but was disappointed when she saw that it was only Charly and Liane on their two Haflingers.

"June!" Charly called out in relief. "Are you feeling better? I was so worried about you!"

"I'm okay," said June. "But where is Nelson? Have you seen him?"

Charly and Liane shook their heads.

"No, unfortunately we haven't."

"And what about those jerks? Have you seen them?"

Again the two girls shook their heads.

"No, we haven't seen them either. When you fell, they zoomed back on the path and disappeared into the fields somewhere. We haven't seen them since."

"Those nasty guys," June grumbled. "If something happened to Nelson, then, then, then …" She took a deep breath. Then what? She had time to think of something, but first they had to find Nelson!

"Should we ride with you?" asked Charly, reading her mind.

"No, your Haflingers aren't as fast as Modena. You'd only slow me down. You look around here some more. If you don't find anything, then ride back to the stable and tell the others when they get back. If Nelson still isn't back by then we'll have to organize a search party."

June stopped worrying about keeping her mother from finding out that they had ridden off alone. Now she was only worried about finding Nelson before something happened to him. She took up the reins again and trotted off without looking back.

After a while, she was out of the woods again and had reached a large meadow. June gently squeezed Modena's sides with her heels and the long-legged black mare broke into a gallop. She took off across the meadow with broad strides as if she understood how serious the situation was and that they couldn't afford to lose any time. June reached the busy road fifteen minutes later and slowed Modena down to a walk. She looked around. No sign of Nelson anywhere. Now what? Should she cross the road? Go back to the woods? June had no idea what to do next. Would Nelson really run across a road where there was constant traffic? June couldn't picture him doing that. But where could he be then? Uncertain, she turned Modena and rode a few yards in the direction from which she had just come. Then she stopped again and turned toward the road. What should she do? After she thought about it for a while longer, she decided to ride back toward Sunshine Farm. Maybe she'd find Nelson on the field and forest path. Because Modena was sweaty, she let the mare walk back. It didn't make much sense to just gallop around the area. If she had known that this was going to happen, she would have gone to "Splash" with the others and had some fun. Instead her body was covered with bruises, Nelson was missing and her mother would find out that they had ridden off alone. It really couldn't have turned out much worse.

Chapter 14

A short time later after Liane and Charly had left June, they met up with Ben and Martin, who were walking with Björn.

"Anything new?"

"Nothing. It's like they vanished into thin air."

"Have you seen June?"

Liane nodded and told them what June had said.

"Oh no, it looks like we really will have to tell Marty the whole truth," moaned Ben. "She's going to be so angry."

With their heads hanging, they made their way back to Sunshine Farm, but they didn't get very far. They heard loud noises again and the two motorcycles reappeared.

With squealing brakes they stopped in front of the four teens and took off their helmets.

"Well lookie there, it's matchstick," Robin leered at Liane as if to challenge her. Marita, who sat behind him, took her helmet off too and shook out her hair. Liane looked from her to the other two boys, neither of whom looked familiar.

"What do you want?" she asked, glaring at them.

"We wanted to visit you, matchstick."

"No one invited you," Liane hissed angrily.

"Who cares?" asked Robin with a grin. "We have just as much right to be here as you do." He looked around. "Or is there a sign around here somewhere that says that the woods belong to you? No entry for anyone other than smelly horse girls and their stupid nags?" He laughed at his own joke.

"I've just about had enough."

Ben took a step forward and looked Robin directly into the eyes.

"You know what you stupid idiots did? Because of you, June's horse is missing. If something happens to him, then you'll have real trouble!"

"Then you'll have real trouble," one of the two other boys mocked him. It was obvious that he was Robin and Marita's cousin. "What kind of trouble, huh?"

"We can press charges against you, for instance," said Ben coolly.

"Oh yeah?" Robin laughed. "And why? Because your

stupid horses are afraid of our motorcycles? That's not our fault."

Liane swallowed. Robin could even be right about that. They'd have to prove that he was out to spook the horses on purpose.

"Besides, Farmer Myers will surely be interested in knowing who's been tearing up his fields," Ben continued, unimpressed.

But Robin didn't let that bother him.

"You'll have to first prove that we rode through his field with our motorcycles. And if you claim that, then we'll just claim the opposite. It'll be your word against ours."

"Don't be so sure about that, young man," said someone with a deep, masculine voice from behind them. Liane nearly jumped and looked in the direction the voice came from. Suddenly a man on a large brown horse came out from between the trees. It was the man they had seen earlier!

"Hello Mr. Kessler," said Ben, surprised. "What are you doing here?"

The older gentleman with the moustache and the short gray hair looked at them sternly.

"I was riding by with Magister when I suddenly heard all this noise. Naturally I wanted to know who would ride through the woods with motorcycles. And then I overheard your conversation."

He turned to Robin who acted bored with the situation

as he chewed his gum. He looked back at Mr. Kessler with an expression of utter contempt.

"The way I see it, this is a case for the police."

"For the police," laughed Robin. Marita and their two cousins joined him in laughing. "Oh come on gramps, what business is it of yours?"

Mr. Kessler got down from Magister and dug around in his jacket pocket until he found what he was looking for. He pulled it out and held it under Robin's nose.

"Because I, as you can see, am a police officer, young man."

Liane gasped and gave Ben a questioning look, but he only shook his head in disbelief. Obviously, he was as surprised as everyone else to see this Mr. Kessler suddenly pull a police badge out of his pocket.

"Please don't file any charges against us!" Marita exclaimed. "We didn't want to hurt anyone, honest we didn't."

"Don't listen to them, Mr. Kessler. These guys ambushed us and spooked our horses so that Nelson bolted and June fell off. On top of that, they totally destroyed Farmer Myers' field and he thinks it was the Haflingers, and now it looks like the Haflingers may have to be sold because ..."

"Please, Mr. Kessler," Liane explained over the din, "You *can't* let the Haflingers be sold. Those two over there," she pointed to Marita and Robin, "go to my school and they just want to torment me and ..."

"That's enough!" Mr. Kessler shouted in a resounding tone. "Now don't all talk at once or I won't understand a word you're saying. Ben, you explain to me exactly what just happened here and then we'll see what needs to be done."

Ben explained in order and very carefully what had happened. The two twins and their cousins stood there in silence and hung their heads.

"Assault and battery, trespassing, damage of property... it looks like quite a bit has been committed here," growled Mr. Kessler darkly after Ben had finished.

"We didn't want to hurt anyone!" cried Marita. "Really we didn't. We just wanted to scare them a little."

"And we're sorry about what happened to the field," she added desperately. "It was so much fun to ride up and down the rows."

"Fun?" Mr. Kessler shook his head. "I can tell you that it'll be anything but fun when Farmer Myers finds out."

"But does he have to find out?" one of the cousins asked pitifully.

"Of course he does!" Ben shouted angrily. "Otherwise he'll keep thinking that the Haflingers did it. And that's not right! Besides, why should we go easy on you after the way you've acted?"

"Oh no," said Marita, "when daddy finds out about this, we're going to be in serious trouble." She started to cry. "Please, please don't press charges against us. Do you have any idea what our father will do to us if the police come to our door?"

"You should have thought of that beforehand," Ben grumbled angrily. "Maybe you'll never be allowed to go anywhere again with your soccer team, and if you ask me, that's exactly what you deserve."

"Please, you have to forgive us!" cried Marita and looked at them all. With her hand, she wiped away the tears that were running down her cheeks.

Liane was surprised to discover that she felt sorry for Marita. She really looked remorseful about the whole thing.

"Can't we talk to this Mr. Myers first?" Liane asked Mr. Kessler. "Maybe there's another way for them to make up for what they've done. We don't have to go to the police, do we?"

Marita and Robin looked at her in shock. Mr. Kessler ran his hand through his gray hair and thought for a moment.

"We'll see," he said finally. "You ride back to Sunshine Farm first and gather up some people who can help you search for June's horse. And these young people will come with me to Farmer Myers to ask if he's willing to have mercy on them and not press charges. But only if they first apologize and promise that they'll never do something like this again."

Robin stood there with his head down and his arms crossed defiantly in front of his chest. Marita whispered something to him and he shook his head. But Marita pushed him over to Liane.

"Robin wants to say something to you, Liane."

"Yes?"

Liane looked at Robin, expectantly. He obviously wasn't feeling very good about himself, but what choice did he have?

"I, er, well, um, I… I'm sorry," he stammered and held out his hand to Liane. When he wanted to turn around, Marita whispered something else to him. "Oh yes, and, um, I think it's really big of you to try to help us out. I, um, won't pick on you anymore – I promise."

Liane couldn't believe her ears. First she had found in Charly a new friend in Washington, DC, and now it looked like all the trouble in school was about to stop? She couldn't believe her luck and could have jumped for joy.

Then Mr. Kessler raised his voice.

"Get going now. Magister and I don't want to stand around here all day. And these things here – your motorcycles – I expect you to push them back, understood?"

"Mr. Kessler is right," said Ben. "We can't stand around here all day. We have to ride back to Sunshine Farm and get help for June."

"Yes," said Charly. "I hope nothing bad has happened to Nelson."

Chapter 15

June felt as if she had been riding forever, but there was still no sign of Nelson anywhere. She wondered how the others were doing. She dug her cell phone out of her pants pocket and tried to call Ben. "The person you have called …" Darn it! He probably forgot to recharge his battery again. Then Charly. But Charly didn't have her phone on either. She thought, why do people have these things if they're never working when you really need them?

She squeezed Modena's sides with her heels and began to trot again. The mare was getting tired and desperately needed a break. June decided to ride back to the farm. Maybe her mother had gotten back already and was organizing a search party. Were you supposed to call the police if your horse ran off? Whom do you talk to if your horse goes missing? June had no idea. She had never thought about something like this.

Shortly before twilight she arrived back at Sunshine Farm on Modena. Marty ran up to her.

"June! There you are, finally. I've been trying to call you the whole time, but your phone doesn't seem to be on."

June contritely pulled her phone out of her pants pocket. She had inadvertently turned it off.

"Do you have any news about Nelson?" she asked tiredly.

"No, I'm sorry, no sign of him yet." She put her arm around her daughter to comfort her. "But don't worry, we'll find him. At least the situation with the Haflingers has been solved."

"Really?"

Marty quickly told her the story of Mr. Kessler, the teens and Farmer Myers who agreed not to press charges against them as long as they paid back the damages to his field by working at his farm for the rest of the vacation. June was perplexed. Mr. Kessler – a policeman? The older gentleman always seemed a little odd to her, but she would never have guessed that he was a policeman.

"And Magister?"

"He's a genuine police horse," laughed Marty. "Mr.

Kessler used to ride him at work. When the gelding was supposed to go into retirement, he decided to buy him."

"But what will we do about Nelson?" June asked suddenly. She couldn't stop thinking about her beautiful white horse, which was lost out there, somewhere in the dark.

"We'll put together a search party now and then we'll head out again," said Marty. "But you should eat something first. You're totally pale."

Reluctantly June allowed Marty to lead her into the kitchen, where Mrs. Morris quickly made her a sandwich. Despite her concern over Nelson, June was ravenous and devoured her dinner quickly, washing it down with a glass of orange juice. Then she jumped up from the table, ran down the stairs and looked for her mother. Alina and Connie walked over to her. Obviously they hadn't heard that Nelson was missing.

"Hey June! Too bad you didn't come along. We had so much fun!"

"That's great," said June and continued on. Where could her mother be? Just as she got to the open stable to look for her, she saw Marty walk out the door of the house.

"I thought you were already downstairs and putting together a search party," said June reproachfully. "Where were you just now?"

"On the telephone," said Marty. "Farmer Myers called."

"Farmer Myers? Oh no! What did he want this time?"

137

"You're not going to believe this, but he said that there's a horse in his field."

"A horse?"

June looked over at the Haflinger paddock and began to count: one, two, three, four, five. "Well, it's not one of ours – all the Haflingers are there."

"The Haflingers are there …" said Marty and smiled mysteriously. "Farmer Myers also said that this time it's a white horse."

"A white horse?" cried June, who suddenly understood what her mother was telling her.

"Nelson? You mean it's Nelson?"

Marty shrugged her shoulders. "Well, we're missing a white horse and there's a white horse in Farmer Myers' field. If we put two and two together, then …"

"… It's Nelson!" cheered June. "Can I have Princess? She hasn't been out much today. Then I can ride off right now and get him."

"Now just a minute."

Marty held her back.

"Don't you think that after all the action Nelson experienced today that he might be just a teeny tiny bit tired? If you give me five minutes, we can hook up the horse transporter to my car and pick him up."

"But only five minutes," said June. "I have to be absolutely sure that it really is Nelson."

She needn't have worried. When they got to Farmer Myers' house, they could already see Nelson in the farmyard, hitched to a post. June jumped out before the car even came to a stop and ran over to him.

"Oh Nelson! I was so worried about you!"

Overjoyed, she threw her arms around his neck. Then she walked around him and felt all over his body. Amazingly, despite his odyssey he didn't seem to have any injuries.

"I'm so happy to have you back again," June whispered to him as she put her face in Nelson's silky soft mane in which a few twigs were tangled. She lovingly removed them, and then combed through his mane with her fingers. In the meantime, Marty stood in front of the farmhouse, speaking with Farmer Myers. After a while, they came over to her.

"Hello Mr. Myers," said June shyly. "I'm so sorry that Nelson was in your field. I'll, um, see to it that it never happens again."

The heavy-set farmer in the blue overalls simply brushed her comments aside with his big, calloused hands.

"I figured it was one of your horses again. You really should give them more to eat to stop them from coming to me for a snack."

June raised her head and looked at him quizzically. What was he talking about? Then she recognized a faint smile in the wrinkly corners of his eyes. Tentatively, she smiled back. Was that really supposed to be a joke? Farmer Myers made a joke? Miracles really do happen!

June and Marty said good-bye, loaded Nelson and drove back home.

"I'm so relieved that it's over now," said Marty as she drove off the farm. "Just a few more days and then camp is over. Riding camp always brings new surprises, doesn't it?"

June agreed with her wholeheartedly.

Chapter 16

"And you have to keep an eye on that girl on Prince Pepper so that she doesn't pull too tight on his mouth. I keep telling her that …"

"Don't worry about it," Bea comforted Marty. "I'll do okay with them. Just see to it that June wins."

"I'm not going to win," June laughed and beamed gratefully at Bea. Marty's best friend had come back from vacation a day early so that June could be driven to the tournament by her mother. She sat in the kitchen with her, drinking her tea and showing off her tan.

"It must have been really hard for you to fly back a day early," said June, who felt a pang of guilt.

"Nope, not really. To be honest, I wind up really missing the horses. When you get back, I plan to take a long ride with Princess."

June and Marty got up from the table and went outside. June had braided Nelson's mane last night and put him in the emergency stall usually reserved for horses that are sick. He also had a light blanket over him at night so that he wouldn't get his sparkling white coat dirty. Liane, Martin and Charly were out there loading June's tack into Marty's station wagon.

"Are you sure you want to come?" June asked again to be certain. "Even though today is your last day at Sunshine Farm?"

"Of course we're coming," said Martin and looked deep into her eyes. "We want to be there to see your big win. Besides, you look fantastic in your white breeches. We don't want to miss out on that."

June smiled sheepishly and pretended to redo one of Nelson's braids.

"It's a shame Ben can't come," she said, to change the subject.

"But somebody has to stay to take care of little Lucy."

She untied Nelson and led him across the courtyard where Marty had already lowered the ramp of the transporter. The white horse allowed himself to be led into the transporter. Once in he immediately stuck his head into a feedbag of hay that June had hung up for him. Then she disappeared down the ramp and out of the transporter and got into the front passenger's seat of the car. Charly, Liane and Martin were already sitting in the back.

"And we're off," said Marty happily, starting the motor. After a half hour drive, they arrived at the tournament grounds. Marty drove to the big field where the horse transporters were parked.

"Wow," said Martin, impressed as he looked around. "This is a pretty big event, isn't it?"

Although it was still early in the morning, many of the riders had already arrived with their horses. June suddenly got a very strange feeling in her stomach. She couldn't be nervous, could she?

Her legs felt wobbly as she saddled up Nelson, while her mother went to the registration desk to find out when she'd start.

"You're down as number 15," she said when she returned. "Now go for a walk-through on the show jumping course and then you can go for a warm up ride."

Marty, who had ridden in a lot of tournaments herself when she was younger, was completely in her element and knew exactly what to do. While Charly, Liane and Martin took care of Nelson, June and Marty walked through the course. Marty had plenty of experience in show jumping and gave her daughter a lot of handy tips.

"Here you'll have to tighten the reins a bit. Here you'll need exactly five gallop strides. And don't be afraid to ride longer, because it's about your style and not the clock."

After they had gone through the course, they joined the others who were waiting with Nelson at the warm-up arena. June allowed Martin to help her into the saddle and rode a few rounds with the reins loose. Then she took up the reins and began to trot. Once Nelson was warmed up, June guided him to the first practice jump. Nelson pushed off well before the obstacle, pulled his front legs in tight to his body and sailed effortlessly over. Then he lowered his head between his legs and made a little buck of joy. The other practice jumps went equally as smoothly and, despite her nerves, June could hardly wait for her turn to come. The show jumping had already begun and she heard one of the riders receive excellent marks.

Then it was finally her turn!

Nelson snorted and jogged as she took up the reins to ride to the course.

The entrant ahead of her, a boy on an elegant brown horse, wasn't at all bad, but he got too close to the last obstacle resulting in a knockdown for which he was assessed a penalty of 0.5 points. He completed the course with a 6.8.

Then June rode in.

"As the next entrant, we welcome starter number 08, June Sunshyne from Sunshine Farm Horsefriends on Nelson."

Nelson impatiently pranced in place until June led him in front of the judges' box, brought him to a stop and saluted.

Then the starting bell sounded. With great concentration, June guided him to the first obstacle. Nelson sailed over effortlessly and galloped in a measured stride toward the next obstacle. The double combination. A piece of cake for the elegant Anglo-Arabian, who floated over the obstacles like a feather. For June the only things that existed right now were herself, her horse and the obstacles. Jumps four and five and then the distance with the big oxer at the end. Five gallop strides was what Marty had said. One… two… three… four… five… and over! Another turn to the right. June rode in a broad arc and guided Nelson to a vertical. She took him up a bit so he wouldn't jump flat and knock a bar. Next, another big change of direction to the left and then a simple double combination. June sat deep into the saddle so she wouldn't lose control over Nelson, who threatened to get faster with every galloping step. He reacted immediately to her cues and allowed her to rein him in for the last obstacle, a blue-and-white oxer. He controlled himself, and with a huge jump sailed over the obstacle. In that moment, June wished she could always fly like that with him. Nelson landed with his front legs and galloped onwards, light and fluid. June rode through the finish and transitioned him down to a trot and then to a walk. As she left the course, the loudspeaker crackled.

"For starter 08, June Sunshyne on Nelson, a score of 8.1 and no penalties. That puts her in the lead in this competition."

An 8.1!

June could hardly believe her luck. She beamed when she reached her mother and her friends.

"Super, June!" said Marty. "That may just be enough for the win!"

Although June hadn't been interested in winning before, she started to pay careful attention to the scores other participants received. And in the end, Marty was right. No other rider received a better score than she did.

She won!

June could hardly believe her luck. She really had won!

She felt like she was in seventh heaven as she rode in to the ribbon ceremony in which the blue ribbon was attached to Nelson's snaffle bit. The victory lap around the green course felt even better that she had imagined it would. She gave Nelson the reins and just let him run. It was a very fast victory lap and the others who placed had to really exert themselves to keep up with the long-legged white horse. Sweaty, but very happy, June finally rode to the exit. Who would have imagined that everything would have turned out so well?

It didn't occur to her that the day was also the final day of camp until she returned to Sunshine Farm. Several cars were already parked in the courtyard and Marty and June hurried so that they could say goodbye to each of their guests.

June even felt a twinge of melancholy as she shook hands with Chantal. Although the girl with the long black hair had been quite annoying, June had somehow gotten accustomed to her being around. Although to this day, just remembering that for a brief moment she had felt jealous of her made June blush.

Saying goodbye to Martin and Liane was especially hard. Even though Liane promised that she would come out on the weekend sometimes to visit her, she knew she would miss the easygoing girl with the fire red hair. And Martin! When June saw him standing with his suitcase next to his mother's car, her knees went wobbly as she walked over to him.

"Hey June!" he called to her when he noticed her walking his way. "I already asked my mom and she promised that I could come back during summer vacation. But in between we'll call each other, right?" While Martin's mother had a conversation with Marty, Martin nudged June over to the bench under the chestnut tree. "I'm going to miss you," he said suddenly and earnestly and then planted a gentle kiss on her cheek.

"I'll miss you too," June whispered to him and was surprised by the fact that she felt like crying.

"I'll call you tonight, okay?" said Martin as he stood up.

June nodded and watched him as he walked over to his mother, said goodbye to Marty and then got into the car. After the car pulled out of the driveway, June got up and went over to Nelson on his paddock. She had taken his braids out earlier, but the white horse's mane was still wavy. He neighed happily and walked over to her.

"Hey there, victorious horse." She smiled and gave him the treat she had pulled out of her pocket. Then she threw her arms around his neck and sunk her face into his soft coat. It was warm from the sun.

"Oh Nelson, what would I do without you."

After a while she let go of him again and wiped a tear out of the corner of her eye. But why be sad? The next vacation would come soon enough!

Horseback riding camp in idyllic Upper Marlboro for boys and girls, 8-16 years of age. Affectionate care, exceptionally beautiful grounds for trail rides and riding instructions with well-trained ponies and horses guaranteed. Lodgings in our picturesque farmhouse. All guests will have their own horse or pony to care for. Contact: Marty Sunshyne, sunshine@horsemail.com, Tel. ...

Julie put down the newspaper. Riding camp with her own horse to care for! She sat up straight and looked at the crutches that were leaning against the wall. Horses used to be her favorite thing in the world. Her big ambition had been to become a famous show jumper. But then she had her accident, and after that, nothing in her life was they way it used to be. How she wished she could sit on a horse again…